FRESH IDEAS IN

Corporate Identity

FRESH IDEAS IN

Corporate Identity

MARY CROPPER & LYNN HALLER

NORTH LIGHT BOOKS
CINCINNATI, OHIO

This hardcover edition of *Fresh Ideas in Corporate Identity* features a "self-jacket" that eliminates the need for a separate dust jacket. It provides sturdy protection for your book while it saves paper, trees and energy.

98 97 96 95 94   5 4 3 2 1

Library of Congress Cataloging-in-Publication Data

Fresh ideas in corporate identity/edited by Mary Cropper and Lynn Haller.
   p. cm.
  Includes index.
  ISBN 0-89134-553-1
  1. Corporate image. 2. Industrial design coordination.
 I. Cropper, Mary   II. Haller, Lynn
HD59.2.F74 1994
659.2'85—dc20   93-31140
                      CIP

Copywritten by Rose DeNeve
Interior design by Paul Neff
Cover design by Paul Neff

The permissions on page 131 constitute an extension of this copyright page.

From the Editors

D esigning a corporate identity system these days often entails so much more than designing a logo and a stationery system. Designers are now being called upon to design for computer screens, to be interior decorators, and to help plan the theme and mood of restaurants and retail environments. The variety of work you'll find in this book takes into account the range that now comes under the umbrella of corporate identity design.

If you're not yet being called upon for such all-inclusive (and often upscale) projects, however, take heart—we also address the needs of less-established design firms in our section featuring low-budget identity systems. You'll be inspired by the elegant solutions designers found to establish identities for start-up businesses and to update the identities of existing ones.

Since we've grouped the work we've included according to the type of business the system was designed for, you'll easily see, and perhaps be startled by, the disparity of approaches designers came up with for similar clients.

We hope you'll be inspired by the range of material included in this book—the very best of the hundreds of systems submitted to us. We'd like to acknowledge our appreciation for our panel of judges and for all the designers who submitted their work for this book, whether or not we were able to include them. We appreciate their generosity in sharing their work—and their ideas—with us.

We'd also like to thank the following panel of design professionals who participated in our blind judging:

Laurel Harper, editor of *HOW* magazine, a leading design journal that specializes in both the creative and business sides of design. With a degree in both fine arts and journalism, she has been writing about design since the early 1980s;

David Lewis, editorial director for North Light Books;

Cindy Schnell, art director at Graphica, Inc., Miamisburg, Ohio, whose work has been recognized in publications such as *Graphis* and *Print's Best Corporate Publications*;

Lori Siebert, founder of Siebert Design Associates, who is coauthor of *Making a Good Layout* and *Using Words and Pictures*; and

Mike Zender, founder of Zender + Associates, Inc. A student of Armin Hofmann, Paul Rand and Bradbury Thompson at Yale, Mike founded his design office one month after finishing graduate school. The work of Mike and his colleagues has been regularly published since 1980.

Table of Contents

Elements of Identity Design

by Rose DeNeve

W hatever their size, businesses today are more aware than ever of the need to create and maintain an effective graphic identity. Fortunately, businesses can call upon graphic designers to help them in this challenging task.

A Continuum of Corporate Identity

Although corporate identity as we know it today is a discipline only decades old, its roots reach deep into antiquity, when potters and other artisans used a particular device to mark their wares, and herders branded their livestock. Even the heraldic forms used in feudal times were a form of visual identity.

Today, identity design is a recognized tool of business planning. Derived from a typically American entrepreneurial spirit, it speaks of a company's desire to stand out from the crowd. Even twenty-five years ago, this was most often accomplished graphically with "a bug and a logo"—a graphic device, or symbol, and the company name rendered in a distinctive typographic form.

At that time, there was a tendency to see graphic identity as a decorative device that positioned a company as modern, creative, reliable. While these messages are still important, visual identifiers are now less an aspect of public relations and more a product of business strategy. As such, they can have far-reaching implications for the companies that develop them.

Identity Basics

No matter how simple it looks, a graphic identity embodies a range of strategic and emotional associations. Its designer must be conscious of the client's business plan—what the client is, what it does, and where it's going. And if the identity is to communicate effectively, its conception must also reflect the hierarchies within the company's business organization.

Although in reality companies most often tailor management to their specific business operations, there are three basic types of management structures: monolithic (companies well-established in a single business or in allied businesses), diversified (which have usually grown by moving from one business into related ones), and conglomerate (which grow largely through the acquisition of businesses that may or may not be related).

Monolithic companies generally use a single identifier for all products and services. Diversified companies use a single corporate identifier and add to it a generic product or operating name. Conglomerates impose their identities, often as a subscript, on that of their component businesses. Well-known examples of each of these types of companies are IBM, RCA and United Technologies, respectively; a search of business advertising and supermarket aisles will reveal others.

Elements of Identity

The two basic components of visual identity are a name and a mark. A company's name is its single most important identifier. It is intimately linked with the company's products and services, and, as business perceptions are built around it, it comes to embody many emotional aspects as well. As the repository of all its equity and goodwill, a well-chosen name should serve a company throughout its lifetime.

Company names fall into several broad categories: founder names (Gillette); names that describe the business (USAir); coined names (Kodak); associative names (Wheels Auto Shops); abbreviated names (NatWest, for National Westminster Bank); and initials (NBC, IBM, GE). The centerpiece of a graphic identity system may or may not be the legal name of a company, but it should be the name by which the company is commonly known.

A company's mark may simply be a distinctive logotype, or it may combine a logotype with a symbol or other graphic device. If a mark is used, it must interpret the company, its culture and its business in an unusual way. The best marks defy logic. They operate on a psycho-emotional level and appeal to a wide audience by speaking to shared human values.

Thus, it's important that a company's graphic identity be developed very carefully. It must avoid any negative overtones, meet the company's strategic needs, reflect the company's style and be unique. It should allow flexibility in application, be easy to use, and last ten to twenty-five years. Moreover, it should make the company stand out in the sea of symbols and identities that floods the business world today.

When To Do Identity

Every business needs to be well identified. A new company especially needs a strong graphic identity to meet the challenge of entrenched competition. But other companies, too, may need an identity overhaul: when existing imagery is confusing or outdated; when a company diversifies or moves into a different line of business; when management or the direction of a company has changed; when a company has been divested, merged, split or acquired.

A good designer learns to recognize when a company's problems are related to its identity and when they're not. If management is poor or a business is otherwise unsound, the best graphic identity in the world won't hold a company together.

The Identity Process

Most identity programs get started because the client perceives that the company is in trouble. The request for assistance may come directly from the client to a designer who has worked for the company before, or it may come as an indirect referral, through a printer or other graphic professional. Sometimes, when a designer suspects that a client has an identity problem, he or she can take the initiative and suggest an identity review. Many clients are not only receptive to the advice of their design professional, but welcome the opportunity to graphically hone their business strategies.

No matter who starts it rolling, a graphic identity program usually consists of four phases: research and analysis, during which the designer learns all about the client; design development, when the actual graphic image is devised according to the previous research; design application, the real work of devising identity standards and applying them to a client's visual communications; and design implementation, or creating a graphic reality from all the solutions and guidelines.

Research and Analysis

Gathering information about the client company—its products, services, management and employees—lays the foundation for an effective graphic identity program.

The best way for a designer to begin this process is by asking for the company's existing identity materials—the standards manual if there is one; printed pieces such as stationery, brochures, product bulletins, annual reports and advertisements; and any public relations or news clippings about the company's existing identity or its business strategies. This material should be reviewed before the first meeting with the client.

In the first meeting designers should establish general expectations and outline how they will work with their clients. The business owner or chief executive may personally want to oversee the identity process or may appoint a management committee. In any case, the ultimate client authority should be the one to make final decisions, as this opinion carries the most weight and facilitates the implementation phase later on. As

Typographic marks, like this one for the Museum of Contemporary Art in Chicago, use a company's name or initials, distinctively rendered.

Abstract marks, like this logo for Kettering Medical Center Foundation, are nonfigurative designs whose meaning is built up over time, through use and association with the company.

Descriptive marks have visual associations with the company's name or business. This logo, designed for a massage therapy business called Hands That Heal, is an effective use of this approach.

for the designer, this meeting is the place to explain the working process and the routine for assessing fees and submitting bills.

Client meetings are also the place to conduct interviews of top personnel. Designers should use these meetings to find out about the company's historical development, its corporate philosophy, its legal structure, and how it sees its markets and competitors. See as much of the company at as many installations as possible during this early phase and talk to workers with different job descriptions. Listening to employee concerns about their company and sensing how they feel about its products and services are imperative for designers in learning more about the company whose identity they plan to develop. In this early phase, designers need to get hard answers to basic questions:

- What does the company do, where, and through what kind of organizational structure?
- What is the management style? Centralized? Linked? Autonomous? How do different divisions/locations relate?
- What is the history, long-term and recent, of the company? What changes are expected in the next ten years?
- What issues signaled the need for a new identity?
- Has the company developed a formal mission statement? If not, how does management define the organization's strategy and goals?
- How are the company and its products or services perceived by its market? Are its products or services difficult to understand? How would it be better understood?
- What are the company's communications objectives? Do all existing graphics look like they came from the same place?

This last question can be answered by a visual audit— looking at a company's graphic communications for the past several years. The audit also reveals where and how the company has been spending its design and communications budget and may reveal obvious weaknesses in consistency and quality that have been undermining the company's image.

Questions like these reveal how graphic identity can best support a company's strategy for the future. After comparing the existing corporate identity with the organization's strategic issues, the client's problems should be obvious: They will appear wherever there is a discrepancy between stated goals (how they want to be perceived) and perceived reality (how they look). The objectives for design development are then built to bring reality into line with stated goals.

Before this development begins, the designer usually submits to the client a written statement outlining the results of the research/analysis phase and establishing the guidelines for the new identity program—how extensive the program will be and its estimated cost. Strict identity criteria should be set at this point, so that the final program will have a list of solid objectives to be measured against. Such objectives might include making the company look dynamic or progressive, retaining past identity equities, meeting certain cost restrictions, and fitting a range of communications.

As for estimating costs, no single rule of thumb is applicable to all graphic identity jobs for all clients at all places and times. Obviously, a large multinational corporation has larger needs—and budgets—than a locally owned small business. A good place to start an estimate is with the client's budget; working backwards from this figure, while cutting costs wherever possible, ensures that the designer won't overshoot the amount.

In devising an estimate, it's the designer's responsibility to make the most of what the client has to spend. Suppliers are the best source for budget input—printers, paper sales reps and sign companies are all used by designers to figure costs. Design fees for identity projects run the gamut from pro bono for nonprofits to astronomical for large corporations with hundreds of applications. The size and extent of the client and the program, the relative clout of the designer and local factors all have an impact.

Design Development

Once the client has agreed to the design criteria and approved the budget, the creative work begins. An identity program of moderate size may include developing a new name as well as a naming system that reflects the company's organization; developing a visual identifier appropriate to the company and its goals; and applying and implementing these across the whole company. Central to each of these steps is the idea of appropriateness—that all aspects of design and implementation be right for the company, its markets, and its stated goals.

Changing a company's name is a serious matter and should be avoided if at all possible. New companies, on the other hand, will need a name that meets the company's strategic goals and also reflects its personality. (See "Elements of Identity," page 2, for basic types of company names.) While there are companies that specialize in name development, a good name can be developed by the designer or a designer/client team, using methods of brainstorming and/or computer name generation.

Developing the appropriate graphic image is another matter. In the past, many designers and company executives assumed that a graphic identity had to include a symbol. But recent trends have moved away from bug-and-logo solutions to all-type treatments, figurative or illustrative identities, or even comprehensive, flexible, image-generating that changes color and form over different media.

Typography, however, remains the primary medium for a company's image, and the designer must constantly bear in mind how the client will use the new identity. If a symbol is the most appropriate solution, it should be memorable, unique within the client's industry, flexible in application, and reproducible in all sizes and media. It should be effective in black-and-white as well as color.

Choosing a company color can be tricky. The colors a client is apt to feel most comfortable with—red, blue or green—are likely to be those that are already overused. Programs that are too rigid about color can become numbing very quickly. Thus, the company color, if there is one, may best be limited to corporate materials, where it has a real role to play in defining corporate style.

Your final design solution should be presented to the client in a form as close as possible to the way in which it will be used. In addition to showing the identity itself, provide examples of a few key applications—stationery, signage, an ad, maybe a vehicle. These will help the client envision how the new program will work and will facilitate selling the design.

How many different solutions to show is a matter of opinion. Some designers produce one excellent identity and swear by it. Others show one but keep a couple of alternates in their portfolios, just in case. And some present up to three different designs, with one receiving the strongest recommendation. In any case, be well prepared to explain how your chosen solution meets both design and strategic objectives.

Application and Implementation

Application and implementation are the longest parts of the corporate identity process and in some ways the most tedious. It can take a few months for a small company, a few years for a large corporation. The important thing to remember is to establish a plan and stick to it.

During the application phase, a new design solution incorporating the new graphic identity must be devised for every piece of client communication. For smaller businesses, this may be a basic stationery package and perhaps a sign; for large companies, it may entail hundreds of separate pieces. In the latter case, the designer will be expected to supply strict guidelines in the form of a standards manual, so that anyone, anywhere within the company or among its agents, will be able to produce communications within the system.

After all pieces have been designed and approved, the new identity is launched. This can happen in one grand sweep, with all pieces being replaced at once, or through attrition—as supplies of pieces bearing the old identity are depleted, new ones, bearing the new identity, are brought in. Few companies can afford to throw away vast amounts of costly printed materials, so most will choose a launch somewhere in between. High-profile materials such as stationery, signs and advertising will be updated immediately; other pieces can be phased in as needed.

Identity applications will vary with the size, needs and budget of the client company. Common applications include stationery systems/business cards, memos, press releases, business forms, advertising, brochures, signage, annual reports, and the company newsletter. Other applications will be more specific to the company's size and business: recruiting materials for a large corporation; operating instructions for a manufacturer's products; tags and labels for retailers; uniforms and promotional items for a service business; menus and table-talkers for a restaurant. The best rule of thumb is to see what a company and its competition are currently using and apply this information to the creation of materials consistent with the system's needs.

This identity system, designed by Zender + Associates, Inc. for a development of luxury condominiums, is an example of a successful solution to a typical array of design problems. The figurative logo, a good way of addressing the problem of promoting something that doesn't yet exist, suggests everything the designers needed to know about the project: The format and color scheme, nautical in feel, reflect the development's riverside location, while the symbol of Cincinnati's Fountain Square suggests that the development is also in the heart of the city. Since the development was not yet built when the identity was created, the designers made every element of the system—including its Trump typeface—upscale and European to reflect the planned look of the development's architecture. This identity system proves itself to be effective and flexible, in both black-and-white and in color, over a wide variety of applications.

Five of the Best Identities

Food Services of America

Art Director/Studio Jack Anderson/
Hornall Anderson Design Works

Designers/Studio Jack Anderson,
Jani Drewfs, Cliff Chung, David Bates,
Brian O'Neill/Hornall Anderson Design
Works

Illustrators David Bates, Brian
O'Neill

Client/Service Food Services of
America, Seattle, WA/institutional food
distributor

Colors Six, black and match

Type Machine, Times Roman, Futura

Printing Silkscreen (background pan-
els); hot-stamping (invitation); acrylic
(give-away signage)

Applications Folders, binders, name
tags, invitation, watches, buttons, give-
away items, displays

Concept Titled "Boldly into Tomorrow," a conference for food-service
vendors needed graphics that would
symbolize the energy involved in forg-
ing a partnership between the host and
its vendors. The basic graphic element—a human figure reminiscent of
American aboriginal art—suggests the
conference's Arizona venue; a sec-
ondary form—a stylized lightning
bolt—relates stylistically to the figure
and clearly says "energy." Applied
against a foil of black and white, the
bold colors reinforce the dynamic
nature of the conference topic.

"Simplicity of style is key to the success of the 'Boldly into Tomorrow' logo, both in terms of message and flexibility. The mark immediately communicates an exchange between two people...a partnership or link. Use of color is not essential to make it work. When color was used, it was also very bold, clean and strong. The style and simplicity also allowed the designer to take pieces of the mark and rearrange them application to application...sometimes dancing around on the stage set...sometimes a single figure on the face of a watch. This ability to play with the parts really conveys fun and energy."

—Lori Siebert

FINIS

Art Director/Studio Lori Siebert/ Siebert Design Associates

Designers/Studio Lori Siebert, Lisa Ballard/Siebert Design Associates

Illustrator Lisa Ballard

Client/Service FINIS, Cincinnati, OH/video post-production

Colors One or two, match (major applications); four, match (brochure)

Type Emigre Matrix

Printing Offset (stationery, brochure); silkscreen (signage)

Applications Stationery system, videocassette labels, brochure, signage

Concept A new video post-production house wanted a fresh, fun look that would also convey its high-tech capabilities. The heart of the identity is an all-caps logotype, which, when paired with different illustrated renditions of the company name, guarantees freshness and flexibility. In addition, a spiral motif, suggesting a tape reel, is variously printed or embossed as a supporting element.

Cost-saving Techniques Major applications were executed in one or two colors, freeing the budget for special materials and repro techniques.

Special Production Techniques Stationery is highlighted by blind embossing and clear foil-stamping; translucent letterhead paper allows printing on the reverse to show through Similarly, translucent papers were used in the capabilities brochure to create a subtle, layered effect.

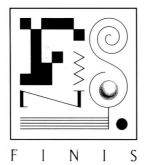  

"The creative flavor behind this program is one of fresh and progressive thinking. The variety of solutions for the type application of the logo takes on a spirited and fun innovative approach. The playful use of thick and thin characters to balance out the type promotes a feeling of movement and visual interaction with the viewer. Each solution becomes a configuration of a veritable 'mousetrap' or 'follow-the-bouncing-ball.'"

—Cindy Schnell

Microsoft University

Art Directors/Studio Jack Anderson, Jani Drewfs/Hornall Anderson Design Works

Designers/Studio Jack Anderson, Jani Drewfs, David Bates/Hornall Anderson Design Works

Illustrators Various

Client/Service Microsoft University, Redmond, WA/leading-edge technical training for Microsoft users

Colors One to six, plus varnishes

Type Bold Sans Serif and Times Roman (logotype); Times Roman, Helvetica (collateral)

Printing Offset (cassette labels, brochure, stationery, catalogs); silkscreen (cassette boxes/packaging, course materials, notebooks)

Applications Stationery system, brochures, cassette labels, notebooks, workbooks, course materials, poster, mugs, banners, T-shirts, note pads, pens, pocket protectors

Concept The software giant began its university as a pioneering, independent venture to confirm its belief in the need for professional training and its relationship to advancing microcomputer technology. Building on a classic typographic identity, the visual system incorporates computer icons, a palette of bright colors, and various textures and substrates to balance the serious nature of the subject matter with a sense of fun and liveliness.

Special Production Technique Corrugated plastic was used as a distinguishing element for course materials and award certificates.

_Microsoft__University_

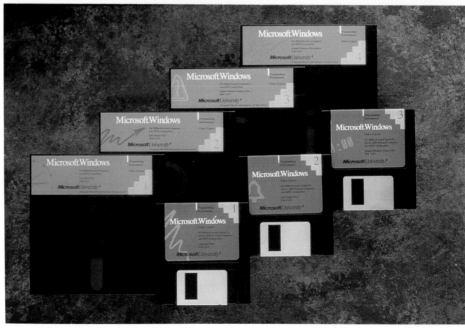

"We liked the simple, clean, yet energetic persona of this logo. It is also a prime example of how minuscule touches can make a project successful: e.g. take away the slide of the *s* into the *o* (in Microsoft) and eliminate the abbreviated bar at the end of the words (which serves as a closure to the logo).and this could be boring. Yet it's anything but. As you can see, the creators took into consideration the logo's use across a spectrum of applications; it works well whether used large, as on the T-shirt, or small, as on the disk labels. This logo holds its own in the total design environment without being obtrusive. The result of all these attributes? A winner for both client and design firm."

—Laurel Harper

Hillside Development

Designer/Studio John Sayles/
Sayles Graphic Design

Client/Service Hillside Neighborhood, Des Moines, IA/residential real
estate development

Colors Three, match (stationery); four,
black and match (packaging)

Type Hand-lettering

Printing Offset (stationery); silkscreen
(packaging, notebook, pen set)

Applications Stationery, pen set promotion, notebook; to be extended to
signage and vehicular and environmental graphics

Concept The city of Des Moines
needed to attract developers for a new
residential neighborhood. The designer
created a logo that could represent the
project both during development and
after it had become an actual community. The form was specifically envi-
sioned as an entrance gateway, open-
ing through the logo's central *S.*

Special Production Technique
The logo was executed as a three-
dimensional pen set and sent as an
invitation to prospective investors.

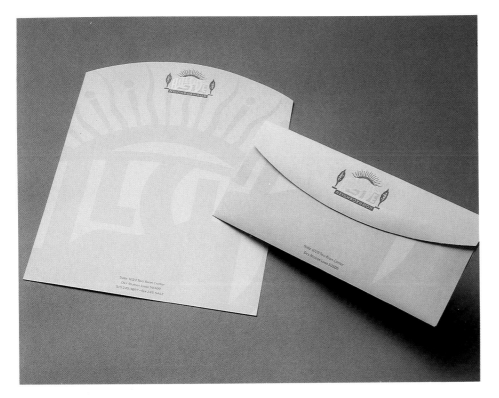

"It's immediately apparent why the judges chose this system as one of their favorites—its designers overcame the difficulty of conveying the feeling of a development that had not yet been built and came up with a classic, yet punchy, system. The metallics and faux-marble textures used in this identity convey the luxury of the proposed development; the rising sun and the trees bracketing the logo suggest an appealingly bucolic location. And note the clever blowup of the logo used as a background on the letterhead system. The overall feeling is one of quality and attention to detail—a feeling exactly appropriate for a new development."

—Lynn Haller

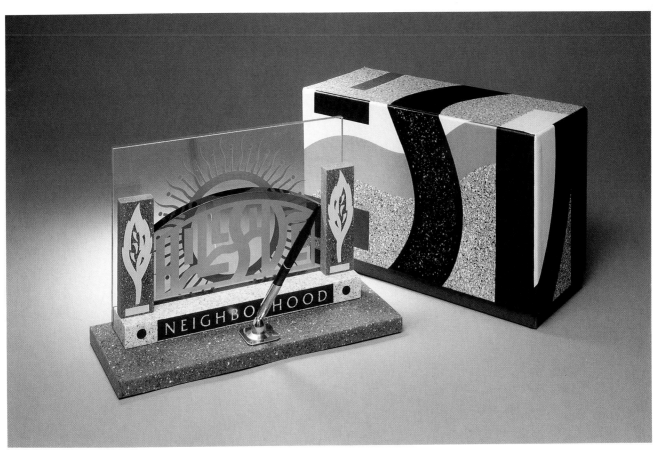

Reading Rock

Designers/Studio Mike Zender, Diane Cartheuser/Zender + Associates, Inc.

Photographer Dave Steinbrunner

Client/Service Reading Rock, Cincinnati, OH/block, brick and paver

Colors Two to five, black and match

Type Univers (logotype); Bodoni

Printing Offset (stationery, catalog, brochures); silkscreen/painted (signage, vehicle graphics)

Applications Stationery system, mailing label, business forms, signage, truck graphics, advertising, brochures, catalogs

Concept As the client prepared to move into retail and residential consumer markets, there was a need for a new identity that would better communicate the nature of the company's business. The new logo typographically emphasizes the materials involved in the client's business and also suggests the interlocking nature of a finished installation.

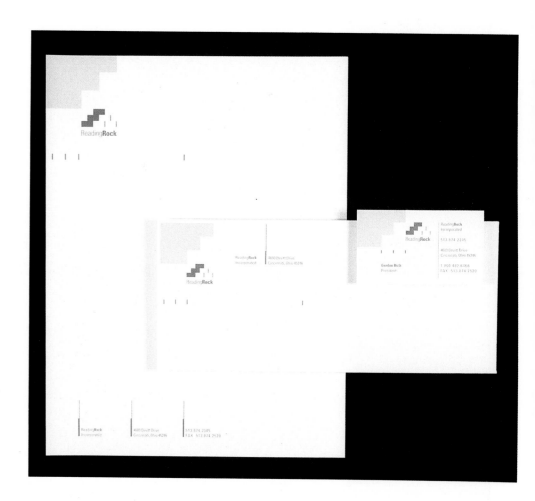

"This system is an excellent example of a design solution which attracts, informs and inspires. The brochure works for the reader because it's attractive, it's accessible, and because the photographs used are inviting and slightly unusual; the whole package presents a subject that's potentially boring in a way that's bound to involve and inform anyone who picks up this brochure. The brochure also works for the client, because it spotlights its product in a way that's so involving—and also because this solution is a sensible, low-cost one. Satisfying the needs of both client and consumer is the hallmark of great corporate identity design, and the Reading Rock system is a winner on both counts."

—David Lewis

Nonprofit Identities

San Diego Museum of Contemporary Art

Art Director/Studio Kit Hinrichs/
Pentagram Design

Designer/Studio Susan
Tsuchiya/Pentagram Design

Client/Service San Diego Museum
of Contemporary Art, San Diego,
CA/museum

Colors Two, match

Type Futura Book Demi-Bold

Printing Offset (stationery system)

Applications Stationery system,
press releases, membership forms,
postcards, employee newsletter,
posters, banners, T-shirts, sweatshirts
and other retail items

Concept When the museum changed
its name, it needed a distinctive graphic identity that would end the confusion
surrounding it and other area muse-
ums. It was also necessary for the new
image to present the museum as part of
the international arts community. The
sophistication and simplicity of the
solution sends the appropriate message and is easily adapted to a variety
of applications.

Special Production Technique
Black heat thermography over pre-
printed black litho was used for the
postcard.

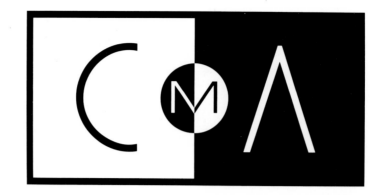

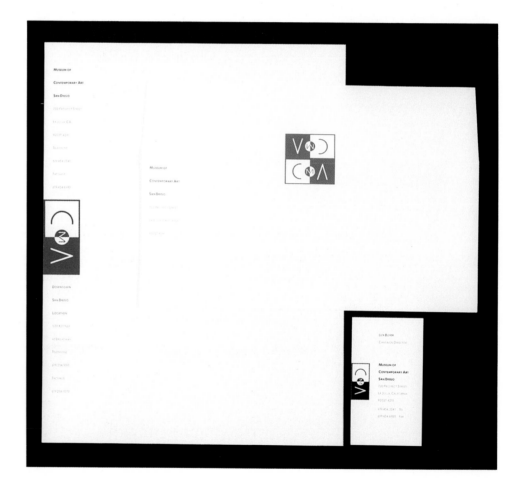

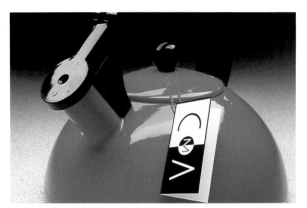

Ballet West of New Mexico

Designer/Studio Steve Wedeen/ Vaughn/Wedeen Creative, Inc.

Illustrator Steve Wedeen

Client/Service Ballet West of New Mexico, Albuquerque, NM/nonprofit organization for bringing ballet into New Mexico

Colors Three, match (stationery); two, match, and four, process (additional materials)

Type Onyx

Printing Offset

Applications Stationery system, invitations, brochure, posters, advertising, direct mail

Concept A new organization needed an identity program capable of raising interest in and funds for its activities. The mark—a visual pun about ballet in the deserts of New Mexico—gave immediate recognition to the group's goals; its application to a variety of collateral materials reflects the caliber and scope of the ballet dancers and performances the group hoped to sponsor.

Special Problems The identity also had to work in black-and-white where appropriate.

Cost-saving Techniques The designers procured donations-in-kind from paper merchants and printers. Materials were used as cost-effectively as possible, with many items ganged on one sheet for printing. Type, colored papers and inks, and graphic illustrations replaced color photography in most applications.

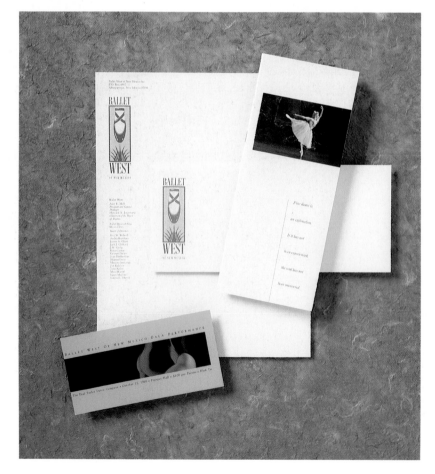

Frontline

Designer/Studio John Sayles/
Sayles Graphic Design

Illustrator John Sayles

Client/Service Open Bible
Churches, Des Moines, IA/Frontline
youth group conference

Colors Four, black and match

Type Hand-lettering (logo)

Printing Offset (brochures); silkscreen (posters, banners); applique
(jackets)

Applications Brochure, poster, postcards, mailing kit, banners, buttons,
jackets

Concept To attract youth to its
national conference, a Christian min-
istry needed strong, sophisticated
imagery. The designer's first solution, a
crest-like image of a lion and a figure
carrying a flag, was rejected by the
client as being too "heavy-handed" and
reminiscent of the Socialist art of the
'30s and '40s; a more contemporary
approach was desired. The second, and
last, solution combines the idea of
"Crusading for Christ" with the sword
of justice; its bright colors and bold
execution especially appeal to young
people.

Cost-saving Techniques Press
runs were maximized by ganging components; by specifying yellow paper for
the poster, one ink was eliminated.

Special Production Techniques
Banners were screen-printed on white
canvas, leaving space for each youth
group to personalize their own. Jackets
were constructed from felt and leather.

Opera Pacific

Designers/Studio John Coy, Corinne Tuite/COY, Los Angeles

Client/Service Opera Pacific, Costa Mesa, CA/opera

Colors One to six, black, match, and four-color

Type Hand-lettering (logo); Centaur (poster); Centaur, Gill Sans, Franklin Gothic, Bernhard (various brochures); Centaur, Gill Sans (postcards)

Printing Offset (stationery, postcards, brochures, programs); letterpress (poster)

Applications Stationery system, advertising, programs, brochures, postcards, banners

Concept An opera company was suffering from a weak identity that did not convey its depth and strengths. With a subtle marriage of earth and water, the new logotype provides a timeless, aristocratic image and a solid foundation upon which to promote the client's dynamic opera productions; the understated type treatment ensures that the logo won't clash with the variety of logos developed for specific productions.

Special Problems With the legacy of a weak identity and a client committee with divergent tastes, finessing a successful new image was a challenge. Once the committee saw the designer's proposal, however, its members quickly came to the agreement that the new mark represented what their company aspired to be.

Cost-saving Technique The logo was specifically designed to be effective when used alone, in one color.

OPERA PACIFIC

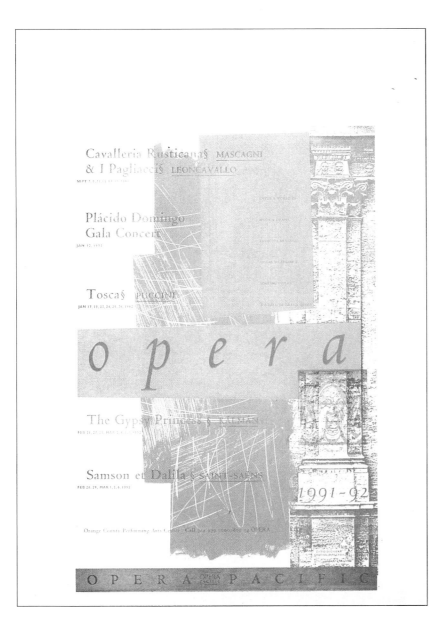

Okinawa Aquarium

Art Directors/Studio Takaaki Matsumoto, Michael McGinn/M Plus M, Inc.

Designer/Studio Takaaki Matsumoto/M Plus M, Inc.

Client/Service Okinawa Aquarium, Okinawa, Japan/aquarium

Colors Various, match

Type Helvetica

Printing Offset

Applications Stationery system, gift packaging, T-shirts, souvenirs

Concept An aquarium needed a new identity to support the expansion and improvement of its facilities. The solution, which surrounds a figure of a fish—itself made from dots—with a sea of smaller dots, captures the environmental nature of the exhibits; its application appropriately integrates both the educational and entertainment aspects of the institution.

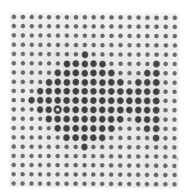

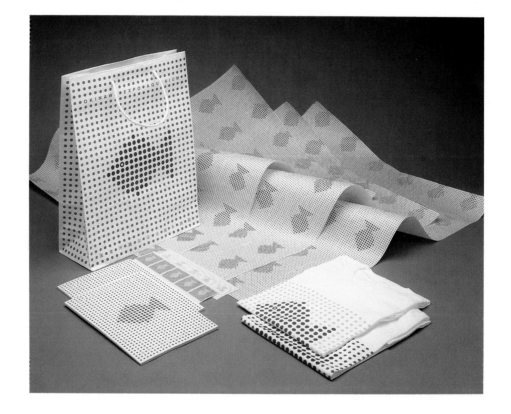

Delaware Center for the Contemporary Arts

Designer/Studio Michael Gunselman/Michael Gunselman, Inc.

Photographer Karl Richison

Client/Service Delaware Center for the Contemporary Arts, Wilmington, DE/art gallery and exhibitions

Colors Two, black and match

Type Futura Extra Black, Futura Light, Garamond Italic, Bodoni Ultra Condensed, Univers 75, Helvetica Medium

Printing Offset (stationery); silkscreen (signage)

Applications Stationery system, signage, brochures

Concept The client wanted a new identity that would both unify the museum's image and position it on a par with other arts institutions in the region. The solution combines a bold color scheme, an eclectic logotype, and a photograph of a classical frieze for a distinctive, contemporary look.

Special Problems To avoid the expense of envelope conversion, they were printed already converted. To accommodate the design, the envelope flap was opened before it ran through the press.

Special Production Technique A 200-line screen was used for halftones.

Budget $30,000 **Cost** $30,000

St. Louis Science Center

Designers/Studio Kiku Obata, Teresa Bollwerk, Kay Pangraze, Heather Testa, Patty Kennedy/Kiku Obata & Company

Photographer Greg Hursley

Client/Service St. Louis Science Center, St. Louis, MO/science museum and Omnimax theater

Colors Four, match (identity); various (environmental applications)

Type Franklin Gothic, Sabon

Printing Offset (stationery); silkscreen (signage)

Applications Stationery system, environmental graphics, signage

Concept The science center had expanded into a new facility whose two buildings flanked a highway. The updated identity complements the buildings' very different architectures while bringing elegance and legibility to a range of applications. New signing and science icons help unify the facility's two sites and are easily adapted to the museum's changing needs.

Special Problems Signage had to aid visitors without competing with exhibits.

Cost-saving Techniques Signs were limited in size and number; anodized and painted aluminum, acrylic, and foam-core board were used for their construction. Much of the silkscreening was done by the museum's own exhibit department.

Special Production Techniques Primary exterior signage was channel lettering, lit with neon and faced with teal Opticolor, a laminated glass that is colored during the day and white at night. For interior signs, layering of acrylic and painted aluminum creates depth; elsewhere, signs were executed with fiber optics.

Budget $225,000 **Cost** $225,000 (design/production)

Cincinnati City Parks

Art Director/Studio Lori Siebert/ Siebert Design Associates

Designers/Studio Lori Siebert, Lisa Ballard/Siebert Design Associates

Illustrator Lisa Ballard

Client/Service Cincinnati City Parks, Cincinnati, OH/control and maintenance of Cincinnati city parks

Colors Two, match (logo)

Type Helvetica Bold Condensed, Caslon 540

Printing Offset (stationery, brochures); silkscreen (banners, vehicle signage)

Applications System-wide parks logo, individual agency logos, stationery system, master plan and plan summary documents, brochures, newsletters, advertising, banners, signage

Concept Cincinnati's city park board was presenting a new ten-year plan and wanted an identity that would both inaugurate the plan and provide a new look for the parks. The illustrated logomark conveys the twin ideas of city and parks and incorporates architectural elements that specifically suggest the Cincinnati location.

Cost-saving Techniques
Computer-assisted design saved time and money in the application development and production phases.

Special Production Techniques
Spiral binding was used for the master plan brochure.

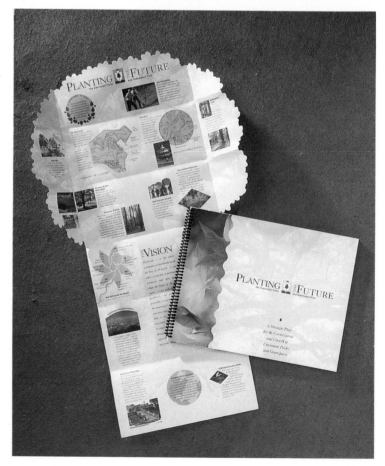

Florida Film Festival

Art Director/Studio Walter Neals/Walter Neals Design

Designers/Studio Larry Moore, Walter Neals, Sean Clinton/Walter Neals Design

Illustrator Larry Moore

Client/Service Florida Film Festival, Orlando, FL/independent film festival

Colors Four-color process

Type Hand-lettering (logo); Futura Condensed (support copy)

Printing Offset, silkscreen (T-shirt)

Applications Posters, folders for promotion/press kit, program cover, invitations, announcement cards, tickets, T-shirts

Concept Custom-lettered logo imparts a unique personality to a first-time film festival; dynamic, cinematic Sphinx illustration is a metaphor for the festival theme, "Film as Art". The quality and consistency of images allowed the non-profit festival to attract top filmmakers and other celebrities, as well as high-level corporate sponsors.

Special Problems The client was an unknown nonprofit in its first year, with severely limited funding.

Cost-saving Techniques All images were ganged onto one 36" x 45" press sheet and run twice through a two-color press. The sheet was then trimmed into a poster, program covers, invitations, announcements and tickets.

Special Production Technique Pocket folders were die-cut from poster overruns.

Cost All pro bono

Tuscon Arts District

Designers/Studio Jackson Boelts, Eric Boelts, Kerry Stratford, Mike Gross/Boelts Brothers Design

Client/Service Tucson Arts District, Tucson, AZ/arts district in downtown Tucson

Colors Two, black and match (stationery); four, process (brochures)

Type Versailles

Printing Offset

Applications Stationery system, folder, press release, thank-you cards, brochure, T-shirt

Concept With a target market of businesses, artists and city dwellers, a community organization sought an identity that would attract more traffic to a downtown arts district. The solution centers on a shooting star graphic as the primary identifier; other symbols for the district's varied offerings expand its sense of whimsy—convincing the viewer that downtown Tucson is a fun place to be.

Cost-saving Technique Stationery uses a black screen to achieve a third-color look; brochures use process-color tints to create the look of seven colors.

Low-Budget
Identities

The Republic of Tea

Art Director/Studio Clement Mok/Clement Mok designs, Inc.

Designers/Studio Nancy Bauch, Clement Mok/Clement Mok designs, Inc.

Illustrators Nancy Bauch, Clement Mok, Georgia Deaver (calligraphy)

Client/Product The Republic of Tea, Mill Valley, CA/high-concept tea products

Colors Two, match

Type Hand-lettered

Printing Letterpress

Applications Stationery system, postcards, product cards

Concept Far from being just specialty tea products, the client's business was about the Way of Tea—the Zen tea experience. The identity needed to convey this start-up company's unique business, centered on "tea mind" and the tea lifestyle.

Special Problems The client wanted a new approach to an ancient product—tea—within a limited budget.

Special Production Technique Paper was handmade from ground-up tea leaves.

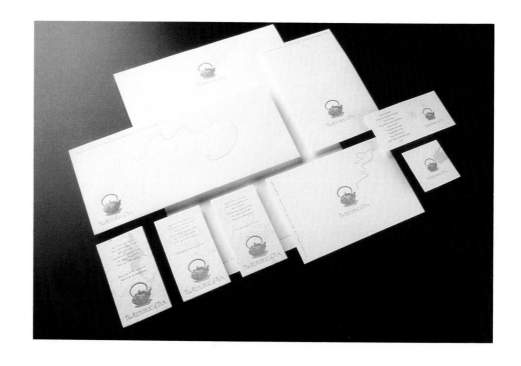

Speedway Cafe

Art Director/Studio Keith Bright/
Bright & Associates

Designer/Studio Raymond
Wood/Bright & Associates

Illustrator Raymond Wood

Client/Service Speedway Cafe,
Venice, CA/restaurant

Colors One, black

Type Hand-drawn (logo); Futura Bold
Condensed (support copy)

Printing Implemented by client;
xerography (menus)

Applications Stationery system,
menus, signage, T-shirts

Concept Located on a high-traffic
boardwalk street, this new restaurant
needed an identity as arresting as its
bold architectural design, if it was to
attract business in a highly competitive
beachfront environment.

Cost-saving Technique The designers devised a menu format that allows
the restaurant to desktop-publish its
own menus, which change according
to seasonal availability of foods.

Budget Trade

The Weller Institute for the Cure of Design, Inc.

Art Director/Studio Don Weller/The Weller Institute for the Cure of Design, Inc.

Designers/Studio Don and Chikako Weller/The Weller Institute for the Cure of Design, Inc.

Illustrator Don Weller

Client/Service The Weller Institute for the Cure of Design, Inc., Park City, UT/graphic design and cutting horses

Colors Two, black and match

Type Palatino

Printing Offset

Applications Stationery system

Concept An existing design firm relocated to a ranch called Red Hawk. The identity had to reflect the spirit of the company, the caliber of design, its new location, and the horse aspect of the business.

Special Visual Effect Unusual application of traditional typeface gives the design an understated flair.

Cost $600 (typography/printing)

Minerva Design

Art Director/Studio Michael
Minerva/Minerva Design

Designer/Studio Michael
Minerva/Minerva Design

Illustrator Michael Minerva

Client/Service Minerva Design,
Washington, DC/graphic design

Colors Two, match

Type Helvetica Black (logo); Helvetica
(address)

Printing Offset

Applications Stationery system,
forms

Concept This identity for a new
design studio graphically represents
the client as a businessman with ideas.

Special Production Techniques
Helvetica Black type was stretched in
Adobe Illustrator to create logotype;
letterhead can be photocopied for
black-and-white forms.

Special Visual Effect The letterhead
positions for addressee's name, date,
topic and letter text are keyed by color
bars.

Budget $500 **Cost** $450

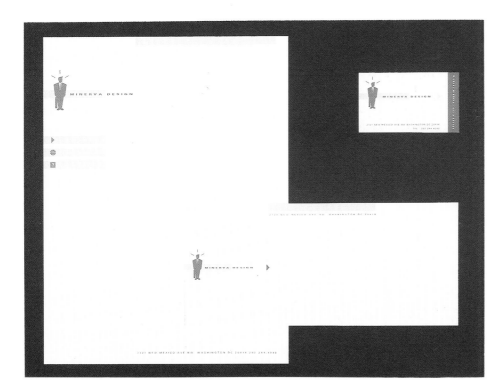

Java City

Art Director/Studio Michael Dunlavey/The Dunlavey Studio, Inc.

Designers/Studio Lindy Dunlavey, Heidi Tomlinson/The Dunlavey Studio, Inc.

Illustrator Lindy Dunlavey

Client/Service Java City, Sacramento, CA/coffee roasters

Colors Four, process

Type Enviro (logotype); Futura Condensed (supporting text)

Printing Offset (stationery/labels); hand painting (signage)

Applications Stationery system, labels, signage, T-shirts, coffee mugs, and other coffee-related products

Concept A new company needed to stand out from the competition, whose identities tended to earth-toned solutions. The client's name inspired the bright, graffiti-like image, executed in a 1940s European style.

Special Problems Although the client had requested a two-color solution, the designer felt a four-color, air-brushed illustration would better express the sense of fun and liveliness the client was looking for. Also, the logo and its applications needed to work for all six locations.

Cost-saving Techniques To help offset the expense of four-color stationery, labels and stock packages replaced custom packaging; additional collateral was produced in one color.

Budget $3,200 (design/printing)

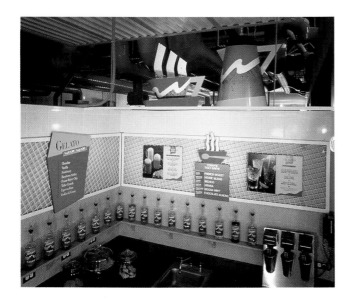

Studio MD

Art Directors/Studio Randy Lim, Jesse Doquilo, Glenn Mitsui/Studio MD

Designers/Studio Randy Lim, Jesse Doquilo, Glenn Mitsui/Studio MD

Client/Service Studio MD, Seattle, WA/graphic design and digital illustration

Colors Two, match, plus varnish on business cards

Type Modula (letterhead/envelope); Futura Condensed Light (business card)

Printing Offset

Applications Stationery system, promotional materials

Concept A structural solution involves the viewer and conveys a new graphic design firm's unusual design capabilities.

Cost-saving Technique Hand-assembly was done in-house.

Special Visual Effect A die-cut and glued business card, printed on both sides, opens into a freestanding paper sculpture.

Cost $5,000 (design/production)

STUDIO

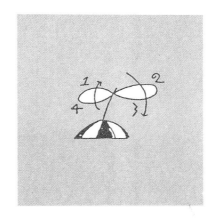

Four Seasons Aviation

Art Directors/Studio John Pylypczak, Diti Katona/Concrete Design Communications, Inc.

Illustrator Jeff Jackson

Client/Service Four Seasons Aviation, Thornhill, Ontario/helicopter charters

Colors Three, match

Type Franklin Gothic

Printing Offset

Applications Stationery system

Concept A helicopter charter company, serving clients from business travelers to film crews, stands out from its competition with a whimsical "beanie" logo carried out in a retro color scheme.

Special Problems Limited funds called for an inexpensive, clever idea.

Cost $3,000 (design/production)

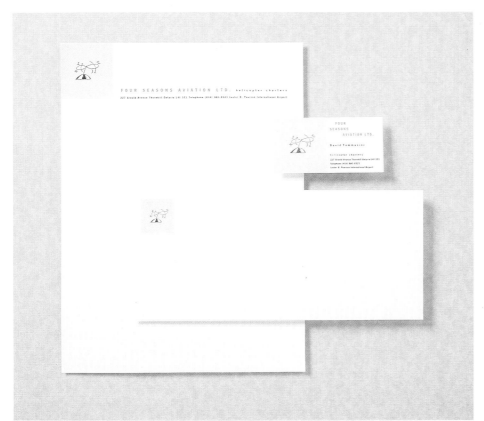

Alamo Heights Pool

Art Director/Studio Bradford Lawton/The Bradford Lawton Design Group

Designers/Studio Bradford Lawton, Jody Laney/The Bradford Lawton Design Group

Illustrators Jody Laney, Bradford Lawton

Client/Service Alamo Heights Pool, San Antonio, TX/private pool

Colors Two, black and match

Type Helvetica

Printing Offset

Applications Stationery system, T-shirts

Concept After purchasing a swimming pool from the city of San Antonio and converting it to private use, the client needed a striking image that would clearly represent the pool to promote membership sales.

Special Visual Effect The clever use of the curved shapes in the logo, which at first seem to represent waves but with closer attention turn into human figures, gives the logo extra visual interest.

Budget $1,000 **Cost** $750 (design/production)

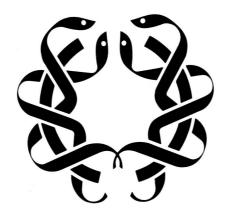

Humana Centers of Excellence

Designer/Studio John F. Emery/ Graphic Design Continuum

Client/Service Humana Centers of Excellence, Louisville, KY/health care providers

Colors One or two, match

Type Bodoni, Syntax

Printing Offset, hot stamp and embossing (seal); silkscreen

Applications Stationery system, certificates, physician and consumer guides, promotional materials, signage

Concept A medallionlike seal—a streamlined, modern version of a physician's caduceus—conveys integrity and prestige for a new health care provider.

Special Problems The identity needed to present the quality of excellence, which the designers felt was met by the medallion-seal concept.

Special Production Technique For certain applications, the seal is foil-stamped, reinforcing its medallion effect.

Budget $3,000

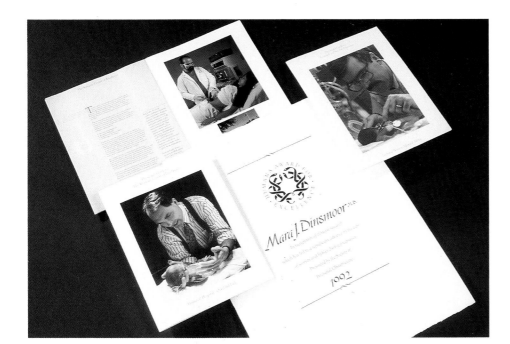

Leading Edge Optics

Art Directors/Studio Randy Lim, Jesse Doquilo, Glenn Mitsui/Studio MD

Designer/Studio GiGi Luk/Studio MD

Client/Product Leading Edge Optics, Redmond, WA/finishing systems for eyewear

Colors Two, match

Type Modula Serif, Industria Solid (logo); Modula Serif, Bodoni Italic (support copy)

Printing Offset

Applications Stationery system, mailing labels, bottle labels

Concept With plans for product distribution, the client needed an identity that could be applied to packaging. The design evokes shapes and elements of various instruments used by the opticians who buy the products, as well as echoing the avant-garde feeling suggested by the client's name.

Special Visual Effects Subtle yet cutting-edge border designs on the letterhead make it easier to keep alignment of correspondence uniform throughout the company; the fully translucent second sheet provides contrast to the gridlike texture of the rest of the letterhead system.

Cost $5,000 (design/production)

Du Verre Glass Limited

Art Directors/Studio John Pylypczak, Diti Katona/Concrete Design Communications, Inc.

Photographer Chris Nicholls

Client/Product Du Verre Glass Limited, Toronto, Ontario/fine glass and tableware

Colors Two, black and match

Type Kuenstler Script (logotype); Bodoni (support copy)

Printing Offset

Applications Stationery system, invoices, tissue-paper bags, price tags, stickers, client information cards, thank-you cards, bridal registry cards

Concept After ten years in business, a retail outlet for fine glass branched out into tableware and housewares. The store had come of age and wanted an image to reflect this fact as well as its elegant, upscale merchandise.

Special Problems The client wanted to attain a memorable image without spending a lot of money.

Cost-saving Techniques The identity was designed for only two colors to keep printing costs low; the photographer was persuaded to work for a small fee.

Cost $6,000 (design/production)

Blackstone River Valley
National Heritage Corridor

Art Director/Studio Melanie
Lowe/Clifford Selbert Design, Inc.

Client/Service Blackstone River
Valley National Heritage Corridor,
Uxbridge, MA/national park

Colors Two, match

Type Eagle Bold, Univers Condensed

Printing Offset

Applications Stationery system,
signage, brochures, guides

Concept An identity for a new
National Park Service historic area
draws on a river valley's past to graphically convey its heritage. The logo represents the movement of water through
a mill as well as through the lives of
the people who have lived in the valley.
Recycled papers were used to convey
the environmental aspects of the project.

Cost-saving Technique All items
were ganged and printed at the same
time.

Special Visual Effect Unique round
business cards echo the shape of the
logo.

Facility Solutions, Inc.

Art Director/Studio Lori Siebert/
Siebert Design Associates

Designers/Studio Lori Siebert,
Michael McCuskey/Siebert Design
Associates

Client/Service Facility Solutions,
Inc., Cincinnati, OH/delivery and
installation of high-end office systems

Colors Three, black and match

Type Aurora Condensed

Printing Offset

Applications Stationery system, uniforms and brochure (projected)

Concept The fact that many of the
client's competitors had unfocused
identities and few marketing materials
inspired the client to seek an identity
that would position the company as the
expert in its field. The logomark depicts
a craftsman carefully assembling the
walls of an office landscaping system;
its architectural feel specifically targets
corporate and design-oriented clients.

Special Production Techniques
The craftsman symbol was enlarged
and ghosted over the entire letterhead
background.

Dancing Desert Press

Designer/Studio Rick Vaughn/
Vaughn/Wedeen Creative, Inc.

Illustrator Rick Vaughn

Client/Service Dancing Desert Press,
Albuquerque, NM/publishing

Colors Two, match

Type Goudy Old-Style

Printing Offset

Applications Stationery system, book
imprints

Concept The publishing company's
unusual name was expressed with a
humorous, illustrated logo that also
suggested the owner's upbeat personality.

Special Problems The identity had
to work in two colors for stationery and
one color (black) as a publishing
imprint.

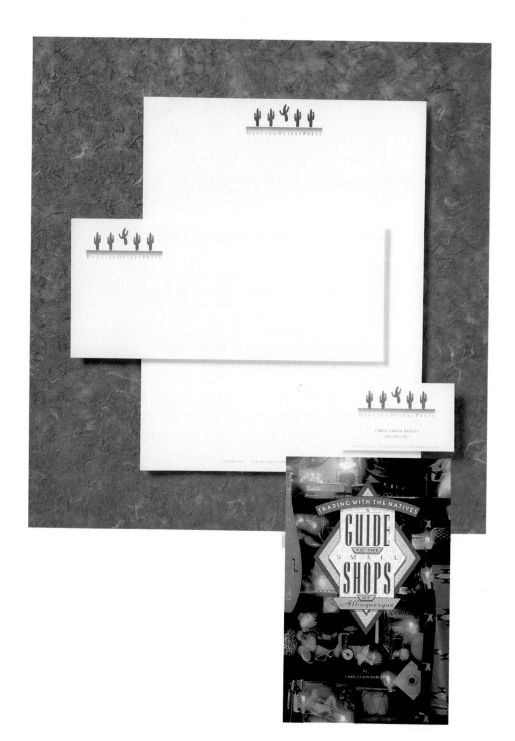

NASA/University of Cincinnati

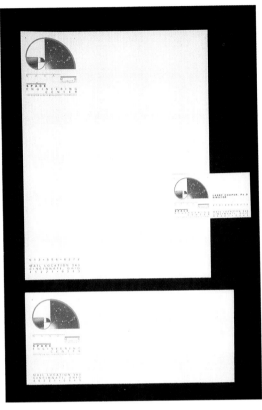

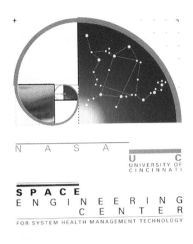

Art Director/Studio Karen Woods Monzel/University of Cincinnati

Designer/Studio Karen Woods Monzel/University of Cincinnati

Illustrator Karen Woods Monzel

Client/Service National Aeronautics and Space Administration/University of Cincinnati Space Engineering Center, Cincinnati, OH/engineering research for interplanetary space travel

Colors Four, process (print media); five (mug, patch)

Type Univers, Univers Bold

Printing Offset (print); silkscreen (mug, signage); enamel (pin); embroidery (patch)

Applications Stationery system, stickers, writing pads, mugs, embroidered patches, enameled pins

Concept One of only nine such NASA research centers in the country, the client needed an identity upgrade that would boost its visibility in the community as well as express the excitement of its operations—research into how to maintain a spacecraft as it travels through our solar system and beyond.

Cost-saving Techniques The golden section engineering symbol was produced entirely on a Macintosh, using Adobe Illustrator software, and output directly as color-separated films for both process- and solid-color applications.

Special Production Technique Having the logo in electronic form allowed easy manipulation for various applications and reproduction techniques.

Budget $4,000 **Cost** $3,600 (design/printing)

Magicmation

Art Directors/Studio Glenn Mitsui,
Jesse Doquilo/Studio MD

Designers/Studio Glenn Mitsui,
Jesse Doquilo/Studio MD

Client/Service Magicmation, Seattle,
WA/multimedia corporate presenta-
tions

Colors Two, match

Type Garamond Book Condensed
(logotype); Garamond Light Condensed (support copy)

Printing Offset

Applications Stationery system,
mailing label

Concept The identity incorporates
elements reflecting the client's business. The square recalls a 35mm slide;
the stairsteps suggest upward growth,
and the small accent square, creativity.

Special Production Technique
The stairsteps were die cut on the edge
of the business card, forming a silhouette of the building where the firm is
located.

Cost $5,500 (design/production)

MAGICMATION

Musical Arts Center

Musical Arts Center

Art Director/Studio Lori Siebert/ Siebert Design Associates

Designers/Studio Lori Siebert, David Carroll/Siebert Design Associates

Client/Service Musical Arts Center, Cincinnati, OH/music lessons

Colors Three, match

Type Bodoni, Bodoni Italic

Printing Offset (stationery); silkscreen (sweatshirt)

Applications Logo, stationery system, sweatshirt, brochure

Concept The client's outdated identity needed a fresh look that could support a more aggressive marketing effort. Finding equity in the firm's existing tagline, "Growth Through Music," the designers gave the slogan new prominence and devised a flowing, musiclike symbol for use in advertising, signage and other collateral.

Cost-saving Techniques Both high-end and low-end stationery was produced; the high-end was printed in three colors on high-quality, textured paper and the low-end in one color on less expensive paper. In addition, in an unusual trade, two employees of the design office received voice lessons in exchange for the identity development.

Railfair '91

Art Director/Studio Michael Dunlavey/The Dunlavey Studio, Inc.

Designer/Studio Lindy Dunlavey/The Dunlavey Studio, Inc.

Client/Service California State Railroad Museum Foundation, Sacramento, CA/Railfair '91 promotion

Colors Two, match (stationery); four, process (collateral)

Type Novel Gothic (logo); Gillies Gothic Light (support copy)

Printing Offset

Applications Stationery system, posters, programs, stickers, pins, mugs, T-shirts, patches, souvenir items

Concept The identity for this museum event held every ten years derived from the poster design, which featured the streamlined era in railroading.

Special Problems The museum's board, which examined the train illustration to ensure its accuracy, was doubtful about the locomotive's smoke trail, which was not technically correct. The designers were able to convince the board that the smoke trail was necessary to suggest the train's movement.

Special Production Technique A combination of cut paper and airbrushing was used to create the Deco-style logo.

Budget $3,500

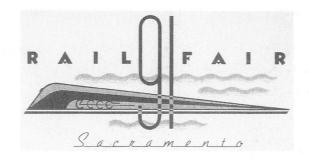

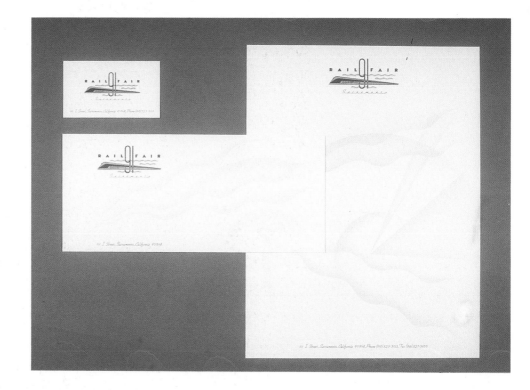

Comanche Canyon Horse Company

Art Director/Studio Don Weller/The Weller Institute for the Cure of Design, Inc.

Designer/Studio Don Weller/The Weller Institute for the Cure of Design, Inc.

Illustrators Don and Chikako Weller

Client/Service Comanche Canyon Horse Company, New Harmony, UT/horse breeding and training

Colors One, match

Type Palatino

Printing Offset

Applications Stationery system

Concept The symbol design draws on a Comanche-style headdress, which also resembles a geological feature visible from the ranch. The horse-head silhouette is an obvious reference to the client's business.

Special Problems Because of the limited budget, the solution had to be successful in one color.

Budget $2,500 **Cost** $2,500 (design/production)

Art Directors/Studio Randy Lim, Jesse Doquilo, Glenn Mitsui/Studio MD

Designers/Studio Randy Lim, Jesse Doquilo, Glenn Mitsui/Studio MD

Client/Service Colaizzo Opticians, Seattle, WA/opticians

Colors Two, match

Type Futura Extra Bold (used with illustrated logo); Caslon (name/address); Helvetica Bold (large telephone number)

Printing Offset

Applications Stationery system

Concept An illustrated logo and a shadow-print of a classic female form for a start-up optician reflect the personality of the owner and her unique lines of eyewear.

Cost-saving Technique Hand-assembly of business cards was done by client.

Special Production Technique The business card is printed on both sides, die cut and glued.

Special Visual Effects The phone number on the business cards is rendered in the format of an eye chart; the two cutouts on the card reveal single eyes from the interior pattern of the two-dimensional card, no matter how it is flattened.

Cost $5,500 (design/production)

Medical Identities

Pathogenesis

Art Directors/Studio Woody Pirtle,
John Klotnia/Pentagram Design

Client/Service Pathogenesis, Seattle,
WA/biotechnology research

Colors Four, match

Printing Offset

Applications Stationery system,
signage

Concept The directive arrow and the
dot represent the company's search for
pathogens—the microscopic causes of
disease.

Special Problems The designers
needed to represent an abstract
process with an abstract solution.

Perinatal Associates

Art Director/Studio Michael Dunlavey/The Dunlavey Studio, Inc.

Designer/Studio Martha Woodbury-Hebert/The Dunlavey Studio, Inc.

Client/Service Perinatal Associates, Sacramento, CA/obstetric services for high-risk pregnancies

Colors Six over two, black and match

Type Calligraphic Roman, Weiss Roman

Printing Offset

Applications Stationery system, brochure

Concept Increased competition necessitated a stronger identity for a ten-year-old obstetric group. Of particular importance was the business card, which serves as a marketing tool with other doctors. The symbol plays upon a classic image of a woman interacting with the dynamics of modern medical technology.

Budget $3,800 (design)

The Brooklyn Hospital Center

Designer/Studio Dean Morris/ Stylism

Illustrator Dean Morris/Stylism

Client/Service The Brooklyn Hospital Center, Brooklyn, NY/hospital

Colors Four, match

Type New Baskerville, Franklin

Printing Offset (stationery); silkscreen (signage)

Applications Stationery system, graphics manual, annual report, patient literature, signage, buttons, T-shirts

Concept An image overhaul for the oldest hospital in Brooklyn uses traditional serif, muted-grey type to convey heritage and credibility, and a cheerful geometrical illustration to suggest warmth and accessibility.

Cost-saving Techniques Large quantities of stationery were printed without type, then custom-printed with specific user information in smaller lots. CAD allowed the small design staff to produce a manual and annual report quickly on a small budget, and the annual was also used, without charts and committees, as a new corporate identity announcement. Signs were affixed to existing signage kiosks.

St. Theresa's

Designers/Studio Ed Mantels-Seeker, Teresa Norton, Michael Beaudoin, Amy Kolker/Kiku Obata & Company

Client/Service St. Theresa's at South Gate, St. Louis, MO/skilled-nursing-care facility

Colors Two, match

Type Goudy (modified for logo); Garamond, Adobe (support copy)

Printing Offset

Applications Stationery system, advertising, brochure, history book

Concept A name change and the desire to include a religious affiliation as part of the hospital's identity prompted this image redesign. The new look was based on client assets and repositioned the client as a warm, caring center with Catholic hospital support.

Special Problems The new identity had to work against a great deal of competition.

Cost-saving Technique Two-color printing utilized various screens to maximize its effectiveness.

Budget $25,000 **Cost** $25,000 (design/production)

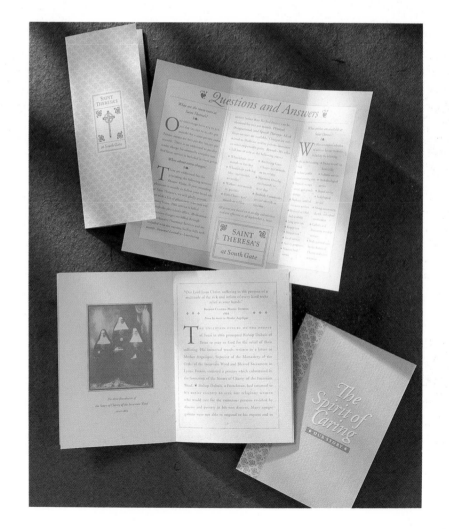

Mammographia

Art Director/Studio Michael Dunlavey/The Dunlavey Studio, Inc.

Designer/Studio Heidi Tomlinson/ The Dunlavey Studio, Inc.

Illustrator Heidi Tomlinson

Client/Service Mammographia, Sacramento, CA/mammography clinic

Colors Four, black and match

Type Weiss (logo); Cochin (support copy)

Printing Offset

Applications Stationery system, signage, notecards, brochures

Concept A feminine image of personal care attracts patients to a new mammography clinic started by a well-known Sacramento radiologist.

Special Production Technique Signage was made from a 5' x 8' black box with a cut-out image and backlit through colored Plexiglas.

Budget $5,200 (design)

The Center for Oral and Maxillofacial Surgery

Art Director/Studio Jack Anderson/ Hornall Anderson Design Works

Designers/Studio Jack Anderson, Brian O'Neill, Lian Ng/Hornall Anderson Design Works

Illustrator John Fretz

Client/Service The Center for Oral and Maxillofacial Surgery, Bellevue, WA/oral surgeons

Colors Three, match

Type Palatino (identity and major support copy); Univers Condensed (map copy in brochure)

Printing Offset

Applications Stationery system, signage, capabilities brochure

Concept When a group of prominent oral surgeons relocated and expanded their services, they needed a distinctive identity that would convey the essence of their specialty without being too literal. It was also necessary for the new image to position the client as a leader in the field.

Cost-saving Technique All typesetting and layout was done in-house on a Macintosh.

Special Production Technique Metallic inks were printed on uncoated stock.

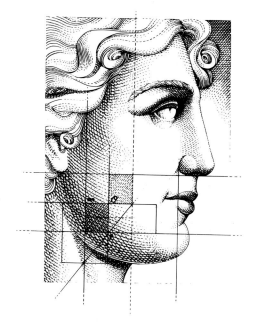

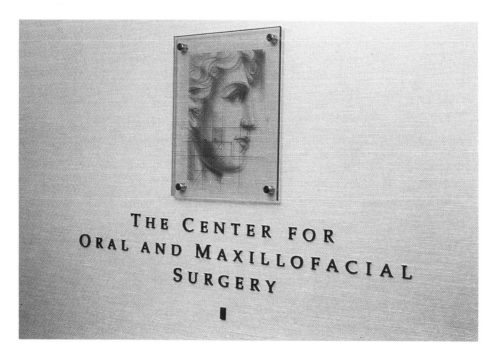

Restaurant, Hotel and Retail

Identities

Hotel Hankyu
International

Art Directors/Studio Colin Forbes, Michael Gericke/Pentagram Design

Designers/Studio Michael Gericke, Donna Ching, Elaine Petschek/ Pentagram Design

Illustrator McRay Magleby

Client/Service Hotel Hankyu International, Osaka, Japan/hospitality

Colors Three, match

Type Custom alphabet in English and Japanese (logo); Stemple Garamond Italic (support copy)

Printing Offset, foil-stamping (printed applications); bronze casting (signage)

Applications Stationery system, forms, signage, packaging, guest amenities, matchbook covers, menus, room folders, glassware, room keys, room numbers

Concept A luxury hotel, located in the new corporate headquarters of the Hankyu Corporation and the flagship of their fifteen-hotel chain, needed a bilingual identity. The client stipulated that the program communicate quality, internationalism, and "the universal appeal of flowers." Based on a system of six stylized blossoms, the new design provides a flexible yet cohesive identity for a large number of applications in both Japanese and English, and is being used as a reference point for developing the hotel's interior design and architecture.

Special Production Technique Metallic inks were used to add a touch of luxury to applications of the hotel's identity.

Pacific Design Center

Art Director/Studio Kit Hinrichs/
Pentagram Design

Designer/Studio Mark T. Selfe/
Pentagram Design

Client/Service Pacific Design Center,
Los Angeles, CA/merchandise mart for
interior design

Colors Four, match

Type Futura Bold Condensed

Printing Offset (stationery); foil-
stamping (executive stationery); enamel (signage)

Applications Stationery system,
internal publications, signage

Concept In this identity update, the
client wanted a more design-oriented
image. The modular, interlocking
shapes of the identifier recall the shape
of the client's building; the clear colors
and crisp letterforms suggest the clean
lines of contemporary design.

Special Problems The interlocking
shape of the logomark demanded
expert registration from the printer to
maintain even spacing between the
forms.

Cost-saving Techniques All graphics and typography were produced in-
house with state-of-the-art computer
hardware and software.

MobilWorks

Art Director/Studio Keith Bright/
Bright & Associates

Designer/Studio Mark Verlander/
Bright & Associates

Client/Service CelluLand, San
Diego, CA/automotive electronics sales
and installations

Type Custom-designed on Macintosh

Colors Two, match

Printing Offset

Applications Stationery system,
forms, point-of-purchase materials,
advertising, direct mail, promotional
materials, signage

Concept As the client expanded its
retail offerings beyond cellular tele-
phones and enlarged its geographic
base, a new name and identity were
required. The designers developed the
name MobilWorks and designed a
logomark with clear automotive
imagery.

Special Production Technique
The type was created on the Macintosh.

Budget $40,000 **Cost** $50,000
(design/production)

Tango Bistro & Bar

Art Director/Studio Michael Dunlavey/The Dunlavey Studio, Inc.

Designer/Studio Heidi Tomlinson/ The Dunlavey Studio, Inc.

Illustrator Heidi Tomlinson

Client/Service Tango Bistro & Bar, Sacramento, CA/restaurant

Colors Three, black and match

Type Trio (logotype); Weiss (support copy)

Printing Offset (menus, stationery); hand-painting (signage)

Applications Stationery system, menus, signage

Concept An eatery with a Southwest theme was converted into an upscale restaurant and needed an identity that would convey the new business's mood and vitality. While the type treatment is refined, the dancing-figures imagery captures the spirit and energy of the restaurant's neon decor, which was also designed by The Dunlavey Studio.

Cost-saving Technique Letterhead is used for the inside page of the menu, which changes daily.

Special Visual Effect The designers retained an original piece of neon sculpture from the interior and commissioned a new, enlarged version of this sculpture to be used above the exterior's front entrance.

Budget $5,500 (design)

Hogan's Market

Art Directors/Studio Jack Anderson, Julia LaPine/Hornall Anderson Design Works

Designers/Studio Jack Anderson, Julia LaPine, Denise Weir, Lian Ng/ Hornall Anderson Design Works

Illustrator Larry Jost

Client/Service Puget Sound Marketing Corporation, Puyallup, WA/grocery store chain

Colors Three, black and match

Type Custom lettering (logo)

Printing Flexography (shopping bags)

Applications Shopping bags, packaging, advertising, direct mail, aprons, T-shirts, sweatshirts, buttons, signage

Concept In order to meet the demands of a changing Pacific Northwest market, the owners of the Piggly Wiggly grocery chain felt the time was ripe to change their chain's name and update its image. The owners wanted an image on which they would be proud to put their family name. The new identity projects a "market" personality while retaining the equity, appeal and visual heritage of Piggly Wiggly.

Special Problems The owners wanted to retain the Piggly Wiggly customer base while upgrading their stores. The designers facilitated the transition by first introducing the new identity with the pig illustration, which appeared in advertising and on shopping bags, T-shirts, sweatshirts and aprons. Other images followed to provide the client with a "kit of parts" for all promotional needs.

Z Contemporary Cuisine

contemporary **c u i s i n e**

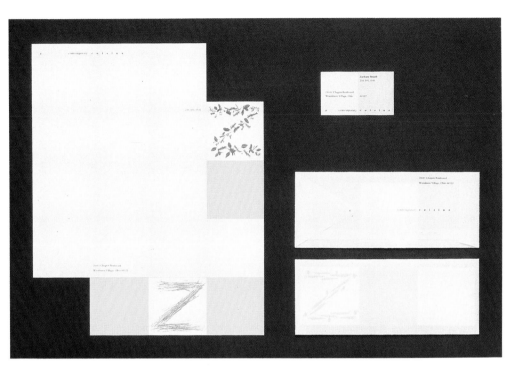

Art Directors/Studio Joyce Nesnadny, Mark Schwartz/Nesnadny & Schwartz

Designer/Studio Joyce Nesnadny/ Nesnadny & Schwartz

Photographer Tony Festa

Client/Service Z Contemporary Cuisine, Woodmere Village, OH/ restaurant

Colors Two, match

Type Bembo

Printing Offset

Applications Menus, stationery system, wine list, checks, gift certificates, signage

Concept After moving to a new location, a restaurateur wanted an innovative identity to support a revised marketing strategy. The current image now reflects the contemporary aspect of the restaurant's food, service and environment and achieves the innovative quality the client was looking for.

Special Problems Between the program's fifteen major components and their associated inserts and updates, the designers needed a solution that could be applied to nearly forty pieces.

Cost-saving Technique Work-in-trade was negotiated with all outside suppliers, resulting in the client spending only 15 percent of the total budget in cash.

Budget $75,000 **Cost** $68,500

Nacho Mamma's

Designer/Studio John Sayles/Sayles Graphic Design

Illustrator John Sayles

Client/Service Nacho Mamma's, Des Moines, IA/Mexican restaurant

Colors Five, match

Type Hand-lettering (logo)

Printing Offset (menu); silkscreen (posters); silkscreen, hand-painting, neon (signage)

Applications Menus, posters, invitations, business cards, table-tents, signage, awnings, interiors

Concept Because the space occupied by Nacho Mamma's had previously been occupied by an unsuccessful Mexican eatery, the new restaurant's identity had to be radically different from the old one. The system's bold graphics, signature jalapeño pepper and hot colors vividly contrast with the previous tenant's identity.

Special Problems The first solution, featuring a caricature of the fictitious Nacho Mamma, was rejected by the client, who wanted the restaurant to be identified more by its food than by a personality.

Cost-saving Techniques Menu-cover graphics were printed on adhesive labels and affixed to die-cut, chipboard shells; inside pages were printed black on fluorescent papers. The designer assembled a prototype menu strung together with twine and finished with beads; additional menus were assembled by restaurant employees. Coordinating graphics were painted onto existing awnings.

Special Production Techniques Flat and corrugated steel was used as wall coverings; chandeliers were fashioned from upside-down aluminum buckets. Decorative accents included a hand-painted snake wall graphic and a fifteen-foot piñata shaped like the signature jalapeño pepper.

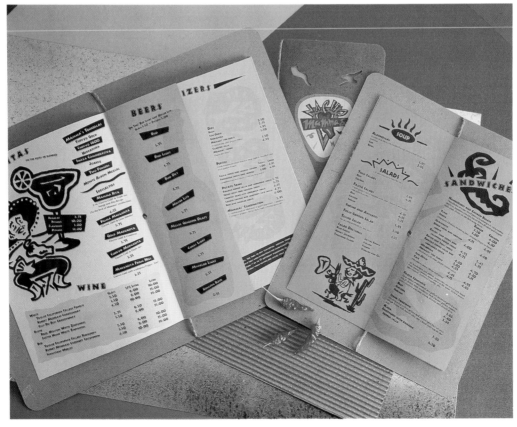

Restaurant, Hotel and Retail Identities **81**

WokFast

Art Director/Studio Keith Bright/ Bright & Associates

Designers/Studio Raymond Wood, Mark Verlander/Bright & Associates

Client/Service WokFast Restaurants, Los Angeles, CA/Chinese fast food

Colors Two, match

Type Hand-lettering (logo)

Printing Offset (stationery, forms); specialty printing (food containers)

Applications Stationery system, fax order forms, advertising, take-out packaging, point-of-purchase materials, menus/menu boards, signage

Concept A growing chain of quality Chinese fast-food restaurants specializing in quick delivery needed a new identity that would support television advertising and a vigorous growth plan. To compete against the thousands of Chinese restaurants in the southern California market, the identity needed to say "Chinese" and "fast delivery" in an exciting new way.

Budget $35,000 **Cost** $40,000 (design/production)

THE ATHENEUM

SUITE HOTEL AND CONFERENCE CENTER

Art Directors/Studio Colin Forbes, Michael Gericke/Pentagram Design

Designer/Studio Michael Gericke/ Pentagram Design

Illustrator Mirko Ilic

Client/Service International Center Co., Detroit, MI/Atheneum Suite Hotel and Conference Center/hospitality

Colors Two, black and match

Type Bodoni Antiqua, Futura Light Condensed

Printing Offset

Applications Stationery system, room folders, matchboxes, laundry bags, other hotel literature

Concept A historic warehouse in Detroit's Greektown area was redeveloped into a suite hotel and conference center. By employing classic typography and olive branch imagery, this identity avoids cliché motifs and elegantly suggests the hotel's name and location.

Cost-saving Technique The symbol was designed to reproduce well in black for certain applications.

Adventure 16

Designers/Studio Scott Mires, Jose Serrano/Mires Design, Inc.

Photographers Various

Illustrator Dan Thoner

Client/Service Adventure 16, San Diego, CA/outdoor travel outfitters

Colors Four, process; two, match

Type Latin Extra Condensed, Latin Regular (both modified)

Printing Offset

Applications Stationery system, newsletter, catalogs, hangtags, packaging, postcards, advertising

Concept In business since the early '60s, a travel outfitter wanted an updated image. The new look creates a natural, woodsy mood, suggesting an enduring respect for the outdoors.

Special Problems After the client said the figure looked too heroic, the hiker in the logomark underwent several revisions until an image was developed that the average customer could easily relate to.

Cost Range $10,000-$20,000

P.B. Pages

Designers/Studio Kiku Obata, Idie McGinty, Tim McGinty, Jim Keave, Jane McNeely, Theresa Henrekin, Pam Buss, Amy Kolker, Ed Mantels-Seeker/ Kiku Obata & Company

Illustrator Andrea Wisnewski

Prototype Fabricators Design Fabricators, Inc.

Client/Service P.B. Pages, The Bookstore for Children, Bloomington, IN/Barnes & Noble/children's bookstore prototype

Colors Two, match (print)

Type Hand-lettering (logotype); Century Old-Style Bold (tag line)

Printing Offset (stationery); silkscreen on acrylic (primary signage)

Applications Stationery system, signage, store design, fixtures, visual merchandising, print materials, gift wrap

Concept A total concept for a prototype bookstore for children creates an environmental identity. "Landmarks" in the form of flying books, new arrivals truck, favorite book characters, book tower and library are built from wood and create a naturally warm and inviting book environment—with just a touch of whimsy.

Special Problems The large maple books and characters were difficult to construct. The designers worked closely with the fabricators to achieve the look they were after.

Cost-saving Technique Basic fixtures, such as bookcases and gondolas, were kept simple and sturdy.

Special Production Techniques Fixtures and landmarks were hand-built from select northern maple and applied with clear finish or colored stain. Book characters were silkscreened black over clear or stained maple.

Communications
Identities

Tokyo Broadcasting System

Designers/Studio Mamoru Shimokochi, Anne Reeves/ Shimokochi/Reeves

Agency Dentsu Tokyo

Client/Service Tokyo Broadcasting System, Tokyo, Japan/ television network

Colors Eight, match

Type Helvetica Bold

Printing Various

Applications Stationery system, promotional items, graphic standards manual, vehicles, signage, billboards, on-air graphics

Concept Increased competition prompted the Tokyo Broadcasting System to diversify its programming and broaden its appeal to a younger audience. As part of the makeover, the broadcaster also sought a new graphic identity. The colorful new graphics aptly represent the new generation of TV viewers in Japan.

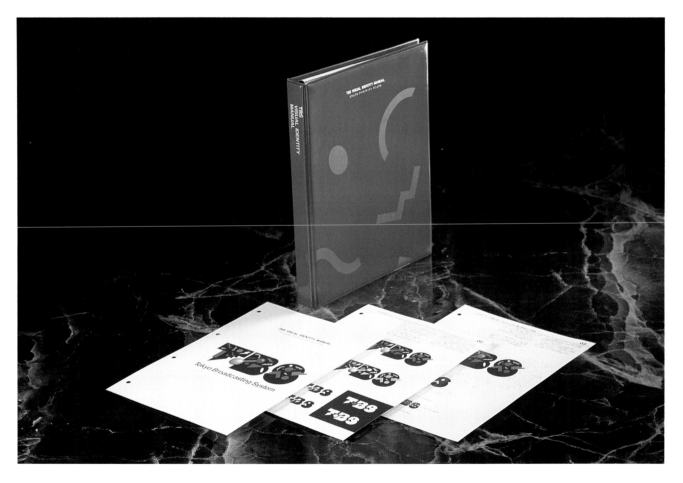

Art Director's Club of Metropolitan Washington

Designer/Studio Supon Phornirunlit/ Supon Design Group, Inc.

Photographer Barry Myers

Client/Service Art Director's Club of Metropolitan Washington, Silver Spring, MD/organization of design professionals

Colors One, black

Type Bodoni

Printing Offset

Applications Stationery system, membership directory, pocket folder/marketing kit

Concept This organization of design professionals previously had no coherent identity. By making innovative use of Washington, D.C., landmarks, the new image clearly communicates design in the capital.

Cost-saving Techniques One-color solution prints black; pocket folder is corrugated paper held together by a printed tab.

Special Production Technique To avoid cliché use of photos of familiar Washington landmarks, the designer first exposed them to several generations of photocopying, imparting a distressed look.

Budget Pro bono

FineLine Features

Art Director/Studio Woody Pirtle/Pentagram Design

Illustrator Woody Pirtle

Client/Service FineLine Features, New York City, NY/film production

Colors Two, match

Type Futura

Printing Offset

Applications Stationery system

Concept An identity for a new film production house turns the first letter of its name into a film clapboard—and unmistakably conveys the company's business.

The Bradford Lawton
Design Group

Art Directors/Studio Jody Laney,
Bradford Lawton/The Bradford Lawton
Design Group

Illustrators Bradford Lawton, Jody
Laney

Client/Service The Bradford Lawton
Design Group, San Antonio, TX/graph-
ic design firm

Colors Five, black and match

Type Futura Bold

Printing Offset

Applications Stationery system,
forms, signage

Concept An identity redesign for a
graphics studio combines the idea of
creative thinking with original illustration—services for which the firm is
known.

Special Problems Finding an image
that everyone in the firm could agree
upon was the designers' biggest challenge.

Cost-saving Technique The job was
run by a small printer on a two-color
press.

Cost $2,000 (design/production)

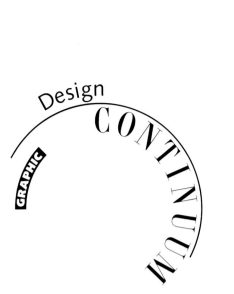

Designer/Studio John F. Emery/
Graphic Design Continuum

Client/Service Graphic Design
Continuum, Dayton, OH/graphic
design firm

Colors One or two, match

Type Syntax, Bodoni

Printing Offset, silkscreen, transfers,
xerography

Applications Stationery system,
forms, labels, checks, memo pads,
promotional materials, signage

Concept A new graphic design firm
pictures its name with an arc that represents a "continuum" of excellent
work. The striking and versatile logo
works equally well in black and white
and in two colors.

Morris Design, Ltd.

Art Director/Studio Steve Morris/ Morris Design, Ltd.

Designers/Studio Steve Morris, Teri Kman/Morris Design, Ltd.

Client/Service Morris Design, Ltd., St. Louis, MO/graphic designers and consultants

Colors Three or four, black and match

Type Novarese Book

Printing Offset (stationery system); silkscreen (sweatshirts); embossing (photo mounts)

Applications Stationery system, mailing pieces, promotional materials, presentation portfolios, photo mounts, sweatshirts

Concept These creators of corporate identity redesigned their own identity system as an example for their prospects. Applied like an artist's signature, the abstract *M* logomark changes color from use to use and is deliberately open to more than one interpretation; its simplicity and vitality express the designers' attitude toward their work.

Cost-saving Techniques Trade-outs with suppliers, direct purchasing, hand-cutting in-house, and personal transport of components significantly trimmed the budget.

Cost $10,000 (design/production over three years)

M O R R I S
D E S I G N

Crossroads Films

Art Director/Studio Woody Pirtle/Pentagram Design

Designer/Studio Jennifer Long/Pentagram Design

Illustrator Woody Pirtle

Client/Service Crossroads Films, New York City, NY/film production

Colors Two, black and match

Type Univers

Printing Offset, foil-stamping

Applications Stationery system, advertising

Concept This identity for a film production company is a visual representation of the firm's name—a yellow traffic sign with one arm of the symbol for intersection comprised of a film strip.

Vaughn/Wedeen
Creative, Inc.

Designers/Studio Rick Vaughn, Steve Wedeen/Vaughn/Wedeen Creative, Inc.

Client/Service Vaughn/Wedeen Creative, Inc., Albuquerque, NM/ graphic design firm

Colors Four, process

Type Copperplate

Printing Offset

Applications Stationery system, labels, forms, promotional materials, signage

Concept A nine-year-old design firm wanted to update its image to reflect the varied and contemporary styles it was capable of. However, trendiness or stylization was to be avoided; the new look had to convey both creativity and professionalism.

Special Visual Effect The use of a curvilinear *V* and a formal *W*, in different colors and designs on various applications represents a spectrum of talents as well as the personalities of the two principals.

Manufacturer's
Identities

GO Corporation

Art Director/Studio Clement Mok/
Clement Mok designs, Inc.

Designers/Studio Clement Mok/
Clement Mok designs, Inc. (entire program); Jerry Kaplan/GO Corporation
(logo design)

Illustrator Clement Mok

Client/Product GO Corporation,
Foster City, CA/pen-based computer
operating system

Colors Two or three, black and match

Type Custom letterforms derived from
Helvetica (logo); Garamond Three

Printing Offset

Applications Stationery system,
brochure, launch materials, product
demo, exhibit environment

Concept The client had developed a
new computer operating system that
used a pen-and-notebook metaphor
instead of the more familiar keyboard
or mouse. A serif logotype and accom-
panying interlocking symbol project a
professional, integrated image for the
new company. Launch materials and
other collateral use "gestural graphics"
suggestive of the operating system's
ability to recognize handwriting to convey its abstract operating concepts;
motion-blurred photography communicates its portability.

Special Problems The client had
originally intended to market its technology as a hardware/software package. However, when the market was
pre-empted by a similar product from
SONY shortly before the launch, the
client quickly retrenched and decided
to shift from selling computers to
licensing the Penpoint operating
system.

Budget $200,000

Ramstone

Designers/Studio Steve Wedeen, Rick Vaughn, Dan Flynn/ Vaughn/ Wedeen Creative, Inc.

Photographer Stephen Marks

Client/Product Ramstone, Santa Fe, NM/floor tile embedded with semi-precious stone

Colors Four, match (stationery); four, process (sample books, brochures)

Type Univers 49 (small headlines); Bernhard Modern (text)

Printing Offset (all printed materials); silkscreen (sample books)

Applications Logo, stationery system, forms, sample books and spec sheets, product information booklets, data sheets, color swatch cards and sheets, print advertising

Concept The client needed an identity to support the product's introduction to architects, builders and interior designers. The ram's-head symbol and restrained typography appeal to design professionals and work to establish product confidence; the presentation package for the product is easy to use.

Special Problems Collateral had to reveal the unique texture of the product and also encourage designers to create their own gemstone blend. Both photo-illustration and close-up photography meet these needs.

Cost-saving Techniques Sample books, brochures and print ads used the same photography. Tiles were photographed in groups of ten, prearranged and spaced for use in color swatch-charts, thus reducing separation and stripping costs.

Special Production Techniques Colored speckles were printed on the front of the stationery to suggest the gemstones embedded in the tiles. Different solid colors were printed on the reverse of stationery pieces. For sample books, vacuum-formed plastic trays (to hold tiles) were laminated to gloss-laminated, hard-bound books.

Padcom

Designer/Studio Vic Zauderer/ Clement Mok designs, Inc.

Client/Product Padcom, Bonn, Germany/pen-based computing technology and form-making software

Colors Three, black and match

Type Syntax

Printing Offset

Applications Stationery system

Concept With a symbol formed from an *i* for information, an abstract representation of a statistician and a pen, this identity clearly represents both the client's product and its users.

Special Problems Finding a simple and effective symbol to represent a complex concept.

SONY Autosound

Art Director/Studio Javier Romero/Javier Romero Design, Inc.

Illustrator Javier Romero

Client/Product SONY Corporation of America, Park Ridge, NJ/SONY Autosound automotive stereo products

Colors Six, black and match

Type Hand-lettered (logotype)

Printing Offset (brochure); silkscreen (merchandise)

Applications Sales brochure, merchandise (poster, bodywear, caps, gym bags, etc.)

Concept Graphics for SONY's auto stereo products and accessories convey the sense of freedom and excitement of pop music and the open road. It particularly targets the client's important car stereo after-market—males in the eighteen to twenty-five age range.

Cost-saving Technique Digital files were transferred directly to the client via modem.

Special Production Technique All images beyond pencil sketches were created on the Macintosh, using Adobe Illustrator software.

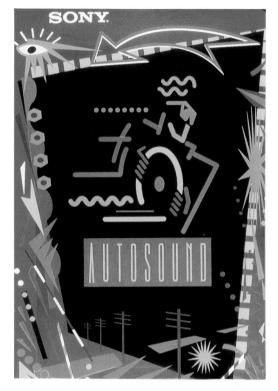

Macromind

Art Director/Studio Sandra Koenig/ Clement Mok designs, Inc.

Designer/Studio Sandra Koenig/ Clement Mok designs, Inc.

Illustrator Ron Chan

Client/Product Macromind, San Francisco, CA/desktop multimedia interactive software

Colors Four, process, with special custom color for background and PMS colors matched to individual products

Type Beaverton

Printing Various, dependent upon application

Applications Logotype, packaging system

Concept The client's previous marketing materials were desktop-published and did not project the image of a serious software publisher. The new look sets a heroic tone, presenting product end-use with allegorical illustrations.

Special Problems The image had to work on the shelf as packaging, as a postage-stamp-sized seal, and as a flash-screen when the software was booted up.

Cymbal Crown

Designers/Studio Bradford Lawton, Ellen Pullen/The Bradford Lawton Design Group

Illustrator Bradford Lawton

Client/Product Cymbal Crown, San Antonio, TX/cymbal holders for drum kits

Colors Three, match

Type Bodoni

Printing Offset

Applications Stationery system, T-shirts, caps

Concept A new identity for a new business quickly identifies the client—the abstract symbol visually suggests the client's product in use, and the type is clear and crisp.

Cost $600 (design/production)

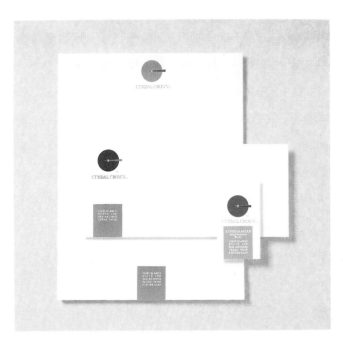

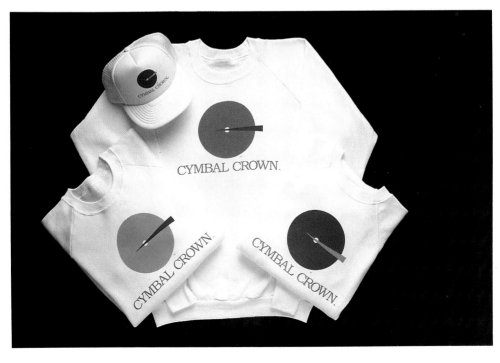

Hewlett Packard

Art Director/Studio Lori Siebert/
Siebert Design Associates

Designers/Studio Lori Siebert, Barb
Raymond/Siebert Design Associates

Illustrators Lori Siebert, Lisa Ballard,
Barb Raymond, Jeff Fassnacht

Client/Product Hewlett Packard, San
Diego, CA/computer hardware

Colors Four, match

Type Bodoni

Printing Offset (all printed materials);
silkscreen (signage, towels); embroidery (shirt, bag)

Applications Invitation, agenda-
mailer, pocket guide, binder and tab-
sheets, notepad, slide presentation
template, signage, gift items

Concept A major manufacturer of
computer hardware was sponsoring a
conference for peripheral developers.
This identity tied in the conference
location—Hilton Head Island, South
Carolina—with the idea of partnership
and used a bright color palette to stim-
ulate attendance. Consistent implementation created a professional, unified look for all phases of the four-day
event.

Special Problems The identity had
to incorporate the right degree of fun
with the right degree of professionalism, and the design went through several revisions before reaching the per-
fect mix.

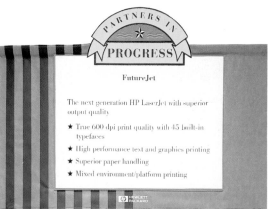

Digital F/X

Designers/Studio Clement Mok, Sandra Koenig/Clement Mok designs, Inc.

Illustrator Mick Wiggins

Client/Product Digital F/X, Mountain View, CA/desktop digital video-editing system

Colors Two, match (logo)

Type Letterforms based on Univers Condensed Bold Oblique (logotype)

Printing Offset

Applications Product identity system (characters); brochure, packaging, launch materials, press kit, video

Concept In what the designers call an "editorial identity," a graphics system explains and articulates the product—black-box technology for desktop video production.

Special Problems Designers had to find a catchy visual handle for a fairly abstract process.

Budget $85,000 **Cost** $36,000 (design/production)

Standard Register®

Art Directors/Studio Mike Zender, Mary Beth McSwigan/Zender + Associates, Inc.

Photographer David Steinbrunner (principal)

Client/Product Standard Register, Dayton, OH/business forms, equipment and forms services

Colors One to six, process and match

Type Times Roman, Univers 55, Univers 65

Printing Offset

Applications Stationery system, forms, brochures, sales literature, slide shows, advertising, signage

Concept The client's existing logo was slightly modified and then systematized to better distinguish products and markets, promote flexibility in use, and establish the client as a solid, stable company with a comprehensive presence in its field. Derived from the visual language of business forms, the updated corporate symbol supplies visual continuity across a spectrum of applications.

Special Problems To overcome any resistance to the new identity from within the client organization, the designers worked closely with Standard Register's corporate communications director in implementing the program.

3Com

Designers/Studio Dale Horstman,
Nancy Bauch/Clement Mok designs,
Inc.

Client/Product 3Com, Santa Clara,
CA/computer networking and communications products

Colors One, match (logo); two, match
(stationery system)

Type Custom-drawn letterforms based
on Helvetica

Printing Offset

Applications Stationery system,
packaging, annual report, product
brochure, corporate exhibition system,
graphic standards style guide

Concept With network management
software, bridges, routers, concentra-
tors and adaptor cards sold through its
direct sales force, this $500 million
company had been primarily engineer-
ing-driven. But with the maturing of the
desktop networking market, 3Com
needed a graphic identity that would
support its transition to a more market-
ing-oriented organization. The new
image creates a strong brand identity in
mass consumer channels, while retaining the equity of the previous look.

Special Problems The previous system lacked brand presence and clarity
in product identification. The new program addresses these issues with consistency of usage and a clear hierarchy
in staging corporate/product messages.

Cost-saving Techniques The
client's internal resources were used to
update existing packages as well as
produce new ones. Computer files were
transferred directly to film.

Service Identities

Bobrow/Thomas and Associates

Designers/Studio John Coy, Anne Burdick/COY, Los Angeles

Photographer Walter Urie (brochure)

Client/Service Bobrow/Thomas and Associates, Los Angeles, CA/architects

Colors One to six, black and match

Type Futura, Garamond

Printing Offset (all pieces); die-stamping (stationery system, brochure)

Applications Stationery system, brochure, mailer, invitation

Concept After twenty years in business, the client wanted an updated identity that would reflect the firm's increased status as architects. The designers redeveloped the existing mark and redefined the corporate color palette, adding textures and images that could be applied interchangeably on different communications. The result is an image system offering an expanded view of the company's personality and its approach to architectural design.

Special Problems Since the client wanted to keep its well-known existing mark, the designers built a new visual personality around it.

Special Production Techniques The designers used a die-cut for the client's brochure, and they constructed a box for the invitation mailer.

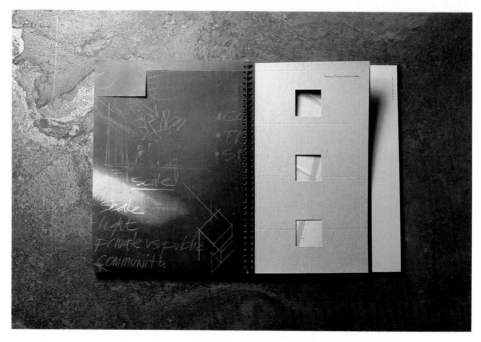

Wild Blue Yokohama

Designers/Studio Richard Seireeni,
Jim Pezzullo/Studio Seireeni

Illustrator Jay Vigon

Client/Service Wild Blue Yokohama,
N.K.K. Steel/C.I.A., Tokyo, Japan/water
park complex

Colors Three, match

Type Futura Bold Oblique

Printing Offset, silkscreen

Applications Stationery, advertising,
collateral, signage, merchandise

Concept An octopuslike mark with
spinning arms, oblique typography,
and a sun-and-surf palette team up to
convey energy and excitement for a
new water theme park.

Budget $12,000 **Cost** $15,000

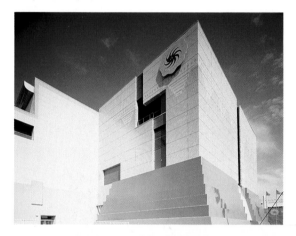

Designer/Studio Darla Haven/Zender + Associates, Inc.

Client/Service ABCO, Cincinnati, OH/ pavement sealers

Colors One, black

Type Helvetica

Printing Combination offset and thermography for all pieces

Applications Stationery package, proposal sheets, proposal folder, brochures, ads

Concept Contractors specializing in commercial pavement sealing and asphalt maintenance, the client had never developed a unified identity. The new look both organizes and updates the visual package, providing instant communication of the client's services.

Special Visual Effect Thermographic reproduction and recycled papers imitate the look and feel of paving materials.

Streamline

Art Director/Studio Michael Dunlavey/The Dunlavey Studio, Inc.

Designer/Studio Heidi Tomlinson/ The Dunlavey Studio, Inc.

Illustrator Heidi Tomlinson

Client/Service Streamline Corporate Planners, Sacramento, CA/corporate travel and meeting planners

Colors Two, match (stationery system); four, process; and one, match (folders)

Type Arcadia (logo); Doric Bold, Weiss, Futura Light Condensed (support copy)

Printing Offset

Applications Stationery system, notecards, presentation folder, proposal package folders .

Concept The owners of a start-up company were convinced of the need for the right graphics to support their image as corporate planners. The designers developed both the company name and its presentation in a modified Deco style, providing a lively image to counter the conservative looks of the competition.

Cost-saving Techniques Layouts were done on the computer.

Special Production Techniques The designer/illustrator used a Letrajet to accomplish the grainy, airbrushed look. The folder was die-cut, with an inside printed with a tint of gloss varnish over two hits of black.

Budget $8,500 (design)

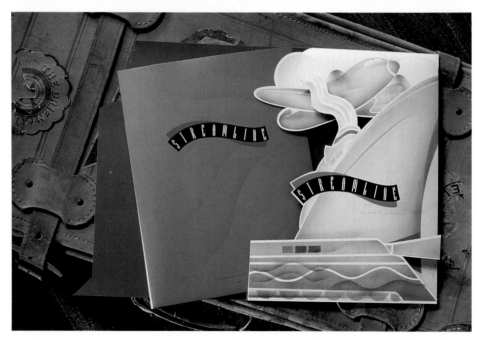

Designer/Studio Nancy McIntosh/ Zender + Associates, Inc.

Photographer Jeff Wolf (brochure)

Client/Service CityDash, Cincinnati, OH/courier, delivery and messenger services

Colors One, black, or two, black and match

Type Calligraphy and Univers

Printing Offset (publications, stationery); silkscreen/painting (signage, trucks, mugs, clothing); embroidery (jackets, hats)

Applications Stationery system, phone-index card, brochures, stickers and mailing labels, large-format envelopes, shirts, jackets, hats, mugs, trucks, signage

Concept Quick response and speedy delivery are the promises of this new delivery/messenger company. These attributes are clearly communicated by the calligraphic "dash" logotype.

US West Communications
"The Race Is On"

Designers/Studio Dan Flynn, Rick Vaughn/Vaughn/Wedeen Creative, Inc.

Illustrator Rick Vaughn

Client/Service US West Communications "The Race Is On" campaign, Phoenix, AZ/communications

Colors Five, black and match

Type Leawood, Caslon, Kabel

Printing Offset (major printing); silkscreen (poster, notebook)

Applications Letterhead, poster, mailing label, pennant, notebooks, name tags, stickers, pencil holders, cards, sunglasses, batons

Concept An employee-motivation campaign uses hot colors, motion imagery and "action" applications to enhance its theme, "The Race is On."

Cost-saving Techniques All stickers were printed on one sheet, on smaller presses with lower hourly costs.

Special Production Technique White silkscreen on the back of clear plastic creates patterns visible from the front.

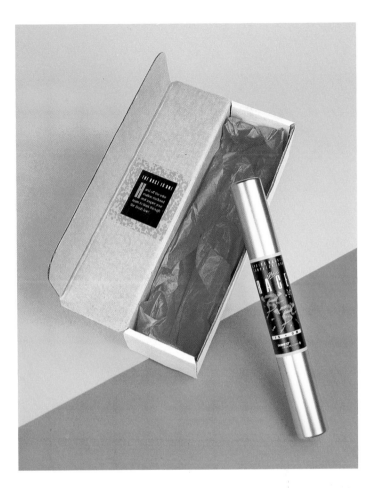

US West Communications "Solutions"

Designers/Studio Steve Wedeen, Dan Flynn/Vaughn/Wedeen Creative, Inc.

Client/Service US West Communications "Solutions" campaign, Phoenix, AZ/communications

Colors Four, black and match

Type Caslon, Compacta, Century

Printing Offset (major printing); silkscreen (poster)

Applications Letterhead, poster, brochure, notepads, certificates, table tent, folders, trophy

Concept Graphics for an internal campaign aimed at employee recognition revolve around a variable logo format whose content changes to highlight various themes. Applied in a watery palette against black backgrounds, the stamp-like identity leaps out at the viewer for instant communication.

Cost-saving Techniques A limited number of colors were used for the whole system and inexpensive silk-screening was used for the poster.

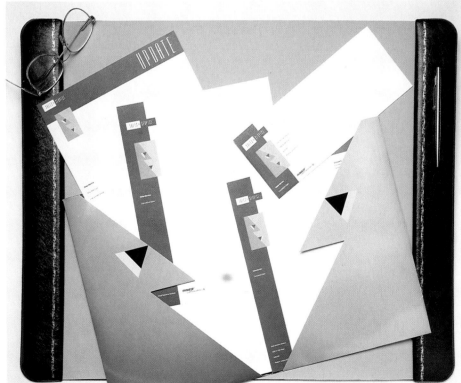

US West Communications Small Business Services "Sales = Service"

Designers/Studio Steve Wedeen, Lisa Graff/Vaughn/Wedeen Creative, Inc.

Illustrator Steve Wedeen

Client/Service US West Communications Small Business Services, "Sales = Service" campaign, Phoenix, AZ/telecommunications

Colors Four, black and metallics, plus varnish

Type Ultra Condensed Sans Serif

Printing Offset (major printing); silkscreen (posters, bookbags, small run materials)

Applications Stationery system, posters, binders, pocket folders, notebooks, note cards and tags, bulletins, training materials, newsletters, slide show, signage, bookbags

Concept The client was introducing a new customer service program in which former order-takers were being retrained as sales consultants. They needed a range of materials to make the program visible within the company as well as to identify program materials. The interlocking graphic suggests people working together; the dual notion of "Sales = Service" and "Service = Sales" captures the program's essence. Metallic inks add a progressive, even futuristic, note.

Special Problems Because the client was committed to diversity the solution had to convey the idea of people working together without implying race or gender. This was accomplished through the use of abstract forms.

Cost-saving Techniques Although the design called for metallic inks, the specification of butt registration allowed all to be printed on one pass. Different items were ganged on the same sheet to reduce print costs.

Special Production Techniques Metallic inks and die-cutting were used.

Food Services of America

Art Director/Studio Jack Anderson/ Hornall Anderson Design Works

Designers/Studio Jack Anderson, David Bates, Michael Courtney/ Hornall Anderson Design Works

Illustrator George Tanagi

Client/Service Food Services of America, Seattle, WA/institutional food distributor

Colors Six, black and match (poster); five, black and match (notebooks); three, black and match (banner)

Type Univers, Bodoni (logo); Univers, Bodoni, Goudy Italic (poster)

Printing Silkscreen (poster, note-books, banners); embossed foil-stamping (thank-you notes); cast brass (trophy); aluminum (signature plaque)

Applications Banners, notebooks, signature plaques, posters, thank-you notes, trophy

Concept The client wanted a communications system for its quality-process program entitled "Nobody Provides Better Service...Nobody" that would both express a company heritage of excellence and also encourage employees to participate. The design conveys the notion of heritage with the classic forms, colors and materials of a traditional seal of quality. A plaque bearing the signatures of workers who took the quality-service pledge brings the entire company into the quality process.

Special Production Techniques
Thank-you notes were embossed and foil-stamped. Trophy was cast in brass; letterforms were sandblasted on glass and marble. Aluminum signature plaque is encased in silkscreened glass.

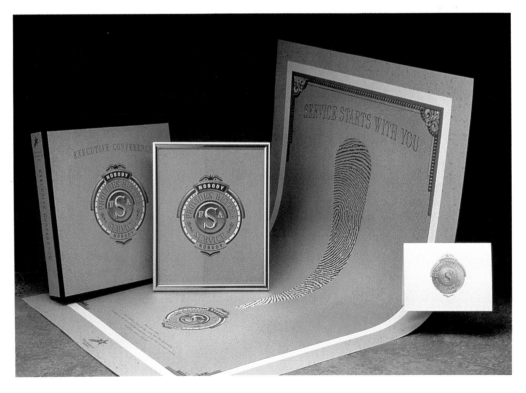

Hollender Architects

Designer/Studio Michael Gunselman/
Michael Gunselman, Inc.

Client/Service Hollender Architects,
Rockland, DE/architecture and historic
restoration

Colors Three, match

Type Bodoni, Bodoni Bold

Printing Offset

Applications Stationery system,
mailing labels, portfolio cover

Concept An identity for a new architectural firm innovatively combines
classic architectural elements and textures and, at the same time, highlights
the restoration portion of the client's
business.

Special Problems Because the marble texture throughout the program was
produced from a single scan, a densi-
tometer proved useful in maintaining
print consistency across the different
papers specified.

Cost-saving Technique A single
scan was used for the marble texture in
all system components.

Special Production Techniques
Colors were chosen from interior wall-
paint color specimens and then cus-
tom-matched on the press; the marble
color was modified slightly for use on
business-card and mailing-label stock.

Budget $10,000 **Cost** $9,800
(design/production)

Gotham Equities

Art Director/Studio Michael
Bierut/Pentagram Design

Designer Dorit Lev

Client/Service Gotham Equities, New
York City, NY/real estate development

Colors One, black

Applications Stationery system,
business papers

Concept A new real estate development firm needed an arresting visual
identity to compete in the challenging
1990s New York marketplace. The
designers developed a mark from a
skyscraper built on the first letter of the
client's name; the form immediately
communicates the nature and direction
of the client's business.

Copyright Information

Design Firms

C l i e n t s

Collateral

Improve your skills, learn a new technique, with these additional books from North Light

Basic Desktop Design & Layout, by Collier & Cotton $27.95
The Best of Brochure Design, $49.95
The Best Medical Advertising Graphics, $59.95
The Best of Neon, edited by Vilma Barr $59.95
Business Card Graphics, from the editors of PIE Books, $34.95 (paper)
CD Packaging Graphics, by Ken Pfeifer $39.95
COLORWORKS: The Designer's Ultimate Guide to Working With Color, by Dale Russell (5 in series) $9.95 each
Color Harmony: A Guide to Creative Color Combinations, by Hideaki Chijiiwa $15.95 (paper)
Computer Graphics: An International Design Portfolio, by The Editors of Rockport Publishers $29.95 (paper)
Creating Dynamic Roughs, by Alan Swann $12.95
Creative Director's Sourcebook, by Nick Souter and Stuart Neuman $34.95
Creative Self-Promotion on a Limited Budget, by Sally Prince Davis $19.95 (paper)
The Creative Stroke, by Richard Emery $39.95
The Designer's Guide to Creating Corporate ID Systems, by Rose DeNeve $27.95
The Designer's Guide to Making Money With Your Desktop Computer, by Jack Neff $19.95 (paper)
Designing With Color, by Roy Osborne $26.95
Desktop Publisher's Easy Type Guide, by Don Dewsnap $19.95 (paper)
Fresh Ideas in Letterhead and Business Card Design, by Diana Martin & Mary Cropper $29.95
Getting It Printed, by Mark Beach $29.95 (paper)
Getting the Max From Your Graphics Computer, by Lisa Walker & Steve Blount $9.95 (paper)
Graphic Artist's Guild Directory of Illustration Vol. 9, $39.95
The Graphic Designer's Basic Guide to the Macintosh, by Meyerowitz and Sanchez $19.95 (paper)
The Graphic Designer's Guide to Faster, Better, Easier Design & Production, by Poppy Evans $22.95 (paper)
Graphic Design America, $49.95
Graphic Design: New York, by D.K. Holland, Steve Heller & Michael Beirut $49.95
Graphic Idea Notebook, by Jan V. White $19.95 (paper)
Great Design Using 1, 2 & 3 Colors, by Supon Design Group $39.95
Great Type & Lettering Designs, by David Brier $34.95
How to Design Trademarks & Logos, by Murphy & Row $19.95 (paper)
How to Draw Charts & Diagrams, by Bruce Robertson $8.95
How to Get Great Type Out of Your Computer, by James Felici $22.95 (paper)
How to Make Your Design Business Profitable, by Joyce Stewart $21.95 (paper)
How to Understand & Use Design & Layout, by Alan Swann $21.95 (paper)
Legal Guide for the Visual Artist, Revised Edition by Tad Crawford $7.50 (paper)
Letterhead & Logo Designs 2: Creating the Corporate Image, $49.95
Making a Good Layout, by Lori Siebert & Lisa Ballard $24.95
Making Your Computer a Design & Business Partner, by Walker and Blount $8.50 (paper)
Package Design & Brand Identity, by Coleman, LiPuma, Segal & Morrill $34.95
Presentation Techniques for the Graphic Artist, by Jenny Mulherin $9.95
Print's Best Corporate Publications, $34.95
Print's Best Logos & Symbols 2, $34.95
Print's Best Letterheads & Business Cards, $34.95
Print's Best Typography, $34.95
Promo 2: The Ultimate in Graphic Designer's and Illustrator's Promotion, edited by Lauri Miller $39.95
Restaurant Graphics: From Menus to Matchbooks, $34.95
Starting Your Small Graphic Design Studio, by Michael Fleishman $21.95 (paper)
Type & Color: A Handbook of Creative Combinations, by Cook and Fleury $39.95
Type in Place, by Richard Emery $34.95
Typewise, written & designed by Kit Hinrichs with Delphine Hirasuna $39.95
Typography Now: The Next Wave, $49.95
The Ultimate Portfolio, by Martha Metzdorf $32.95
Using Type Right, by Philip Brady $18.95 (paper)